I0017692

Table of Contents

Chapter 1: Introduction to Advanced SFML Techniques

Section 1.1: Exploring the Scope of Advanced SFML Programming

In this section, we will delve into the exciting world of advanced SFML programming and explore the extensive scope it offers for multimedia application development. Advanced SFML techniques open up a realm of possibilities for creating highly interactive and visually appealing applications that go beyond the basics.

SFML, the Simple and Fast Multimedia Library, is a versatile and powerful C++ library that provides developers with the tools they need to create multimedia applications. While SFML is known for its ease of use, it also boasts a wide range of advanced features that enable developers to create sophisticated and feature-rich applications.

Advanced SFML programming is not limited to any specific type of application; it extends its reach to various domains, including but not limited to:

1. **Game Development:** SFML is a popular choice for 2D game development, and advanced techniques can take your games to the next level with enhanced graphics, input handling, and audio effects.

2. **Multimedia Players:** You can build multimedia players with advanced features such as custom UIs, playlist management, and cross-platform deployment.

3. **Drawing Applications:** Advanced drawing applications can benefit from features like complex drawing tools, layer management, and cross-platform compatibility.

4. **Audio Processing:** SFML allows real-time audio synthesis, custom audio effects, and interactive music generation, making it a valuable tool for audio processing applications.

5. **Networking:** For networked applications and games, SFML provides capabilities for implementing networked gameplay and handling security considerations.

6. **Augmented Reality (AR) and Virtual Reality (VR):** SFML can be used to develop cross-platform AR and VR applications, offering users immersive experiences.

This section will provide an overview of the exciting journey that awaits you in this book as we explore the advanced capabilities of SFML. We'll delve into each of these application domains in subsequent chapters, equipping you with the knowledge and skills to create cutting-edge applications.

But before we dive deeper into these domains, let's understand why SFML is an excellent choice for advanced development and how it can simplify the creation of cross-platform applications that push the boundaries of multimedia programming.

Section 1.2: Leveraging Advanced SFML for Multimedia Applications

In this section, we will explore how advanced SFML can be leveraged to create a wide range of multimedia applications. SFML, with its rich set of features, is an excellent choice for developing multimedia applications that encompass graphics, audio, and user interaction.

The Multimedia Power of SFML

SFML is designed to handle multimedia tasks efficiently. It provides native support for various multimedia elements, making it a versatile choice for multimedia applications:

1. **Graphics:** SFML offers robust 2D graphics capabilities, including sprite rendering, texture handling, and customizable rendering using shaders. This makes it ideal for creating visually appealing multimedia interfaces and games.

2. **Audio:** SFML supports audio playback and manipulation, including the ability to play sound effects, music, and real-time audio synthesis. This makes it suitable for multimedia players, audio processing applications, and games with immersive soundscapes.

3. **Input Handling:** SFML simplifies input handling with support for keyboard, mouse, and joystick input. Advanced input features, such as multitouch and gesture recognition, enable rich user interactions in multimedia applications.

4. **Cross-Platform Compatibility:** SFML is designed to work seamlessly across multiple platforms, including Windows, macOS, Linux, iOS, and Android. This cross-platform support is crucial for reaching a wide audience with your multimedia applications.

Building Multimedia Players

One common use case for advanced SFML programming is the development of multimedia players. These applications can play a variety of media types, including audio and video, and often include features like playlist management, custom user interfaces, and cross-platform deployment.

Let's outline the key components of building a multimedia player with advanced SFML techniques:

1. **Audio and Video Playback:** Advanced SFML allows you to seamlessly integrate audio and video playback into your multimedia player. You can load and play media files in various formats, control playback speed, and implement features like seeking and volume control.

2. **Playlist and Navigation Features:** To enhance user experience, implement playlist management features. Users can create, edit, and save playlists, navigate between media items, and control playback order.

3. **Custom User Interface:** Design a user-friendly and visually appealing custom user interface (UI) for your multimedia player. SFML's graphics capabilities enable you to create custom buttons, sliders, and other UI elements to control playback and manage playlists.

4. **Cross-Platform Deployment:** Ensure that your multimedia player can run smoothly on different platforms. Advanced SFML simplifies the process of deploying your application on Windows, macOS, Linux, iOS, and Android.

To illustrate, here's a simplified code snippet in C++ that demonstrates how to create a basic audio player using SFML:

```cpp
#include <SFML/Audio.hpp>
#include <SFML/Graphics.hpp>

int main() {
    // Initialize SFML components
    sf::RenderWindow window(sf::VideoMode(800, 600), "SFML Audio Player");
    sf::Music music;

    // Load audio file
    if (!music.openFromFile("sample.ogg")) {
        // Handle file loading error
        return 1;
    }

    // Play the audio
    music.play();

    // Main loop
    while (window.isOpen()) {
        sf::Event event;
        while (window.pollEvent(event)) {
            if (event.type == sf::Event::Closed) {
                window.close();
            }
        }

        window.clear();
        // Draw UI elements and controls here
        window.display();
    }

    return 0;
}
```

This code sets up a basic audio player window and plays an audio file using SFML's sf::Music class. While this is a simplified example, it illustrates the core concepts of creating a multimedia player with SFML.

In the upcoming chapters, we will delve into more advanced techniques for building multimedia applications and explore how SFML can empower you to create engaging and cross-platform multimedia experiences.

Section 1.3: Cross-Platform Development with SFML

In this section, we will explore the significance of cross-platform development with SFML and how it simplifies the process of creating multimedia applications that can run seamlessly on various operating systems. Cross-platform development is a crucial aspect of modern software engineering, as it allows developers to reach a broader audience and maximize the impact of their applications.

The Challenge of Platform Diversity

Developing software for multiple platforms presents unique challenges due to the diversity of operating systems, hardware configurations, and software dependencies. These challenges can include:

1. **OS Compatibility:** Different operating systems have varying APIs, system libraries, and behaviors. Writing platform-specific code for each OS can be time-consuming and error-prone.

2. **Hardware Variation:** Hardware components such as graphics cards, processors, and input devices can vary significantly between platforms. Ensuring that your application performs well on all hardware configurations is a complex task.

3. **Library Dependencies:** Software libraries and dependencies may differ between platforms. Managing these dependencies and ensuring they work correctly on each platform can be a headache.

4. **User Experience:** Users expect applications to look and behave consistently across platforms. Inconsistent user experiences can lead to frustration and decreased user satisfaction.

SFML's Cross-Platform Support

SFML is designed with cross-platform development in mind, making it an excellent choice for developers who want to create applications that can reach a wide audience. Here's how SFML simplifies cross-platform development:

1. **Platform Abstraction:** SFML provides a consistent and abstracted interface for interacting with various operating systems. You can write code that targets SFML's API, and SFML takes care of the platform-specific details.

2. **Hardware Independence:** SFML abstracts hardware interactions, ensuring that your application runs smoothly across different hardware configurations. Whether it's rendering graphics or handling input, SFML handles the intricacies.

3. **Library Management:** SFML bundles its dependencies and provides a unified interface to them. This means you don't have to worry about managing external libraries and can focus on your application's logic.

4. **Cross-Platform Compatibility:** SFML applications can be compiled and run on Windows, macOS, Linux, iOS, and Android with minimal platform-specific code. This flexibility simplifies deployment to multiple platforms.

Writing Cross-Platform Code

To illustrate SFML's cross-platform capabilities, let's take a look at a simple code snippet that creates a cross-platform window using SFML:

```cpp
#include <SFML/Graphics.hpp>

int main() {
    sf::RenderWindow window(sf::VideoMode(800, 600), "Cross-Platform SFML Window");

    while (window.isOpen()) {
        sf::Event event;
        while (window.pollEvent(event)) {
            if (event.type == sf::Event::Closed) {
                window.close();
            }
        }

        window.clear();
        // Draw your application content here
        window.display();
    }

    return 0;
}
```

This code creates a window that can run on various platforms without modification. The SFML library abstracts the platform-specific window creation and event handling, allowing you to focus on your application's functionality.

In the upcoming chapters, we will explore more advanced aspects of cross-platform development with SFML, including strategies for handling platform-specific features and considerations. Understanding how to navigate the challenges of cross-platform development is essential for creating successful multimedia applications that can thrive in diverse computing environments.

Section 1.4: Building Multi-Chapter Projects with SFML

In this section, we will delve into the concept of building multi-chapter projects with SFML. While individual SFML projects can be powerful on their own, there are situations where you may need to create larger, interconnected projects that span multiple chapters or sections of a book. Multi-chapter projects allow you to create complex applications or games with a cohesive user experience, sharing assets, resources, and functionality across different parts of the project.

Benefits of Multi-Chapter Projects

Building multi-chapter projects with SFML offers several advantages:

1. **Consistency:** When you work on a project that spans multiple chapters, you can maintain a consistent user interface and design throughout the application. This consistency contributes to a polished and professional user experience.

2. **Reusability:** Multi-chapter projects enable you to reuse code, assets, and resources efficiently. This can save development time and reduce redundancy in your codebase.

3. **Complexity Handling:** Some projects, especially games or multimedia applications, can become quite complex. Breaking them into manageable chapters makes it easier to handle and understand the various components and features.

4. **Team Collaboration:** In collaborative development environments, different team members can focus on specific chapters or sections of the project, enhancing productivity and specialization.

Designing Multi-Chapter Projects

Creating a multi-chapter project with SFML involves careful planning and design. Here are some key considerations:

1. **Project Structure:** Plan how your project will be organized across chapters. Consider creating a folder structure that separates assets, code, and resources for each chapter. This makes it easier to manage and maintain the project.

2. **Asset Management:** Decide how assets such as graphics, audio files, and data will be shared across chapters. You may want a centralized asset management system to ensure consistency.

3. **Code Modularization:** Design your code with modularity in mind. Identify common functionality that can be encapsulated in reusable modules or libraries. This simplifies code maintenance and promotes code reuse.

4. **Chapter Dependencies:** Understand the dependencies between chapters. Ensure that each chapter can function independently but can also interact with other chapters when necessary.

Code Example: Shared Asset Loading

Let's consider a simple example of how to share assets across chapters using SFML. Suppose you have a game project with multiple levels, each represented by a separate chapter. You want to load and display level-specific textures while reusing common assets like fonts and sound effects.

```
#include <SFML/Graphics.hpp>

// Common assets used across chapters
sf::Font commonFont;
sf::SoundBuffer commonSound;

void loadCommonAssets() {
    if (!commonFont.loadFromFile("common_font.ttf")) {
        // Handle font loading error
    }

    if (!commonSound.loadFromFile("common_sound.wav")) {
        // Handle sound loading error
    }
}

int main() {
    sf::RenderWindow window(sf::VideoMode(800, 600), "Multi-Chapter SFML Proj
ect");

    // Load common assets
    loadCommonAssets();

    while (window.isOpen()) {
        sf::Event event;
        while (window.pollEvent(event)) {
            if (event.type == sf::Event::Closed) {
                window.close();
            }
        }

        window.clear();
        // Draw and interact with the current chapter's content
        window.display();
    }

    return 0;
}
```

In this example, we load common assets like fonts and sound effects in a centralized function `loadCommonAssets()`. Each chapter of the project can then use these assets as needed without duplicating the loading process.

Multi-chapter projects with SFML provide a structured approach to building complex multimedia applications or games. By carefully designing your project structure and considering code modularity and asset management, you can create cohesive and efficient applications that benefit from the advantages of a multi-chapter approach.

Section 1.5: Abstracting SFML for Modular Development

In this section, we will explore the concept of abstracting SFML for modular development. Abstracting SFML involves creating a layer of separation between your application's core logic and the SFML library. This abstraction allows for more modular and maintainable code, making it easier to work on large-scale projects and collaborate with team members.

The Need for Abstraction

Abstraction is a fundamental principle in software engineering, and it plays a crucial role in building complex applications with SFML. Here are some reasons why abstracting SFML is beneficial:

1. **Modularity:** By abstracting SFML functionality into separate modules or classes, you can isolate specific features and components. This modularity makes it easier to develop, test, and maintain individual parts of your application.

2. **Code Reusability:** Abstracted SFML code can be reused across different parts of your project. For example, if you've created a custom button UI element with SFML, you can use it in various chapters or sections of your application.

3. **Collaboration:** When working on projects with multiple team members, abstracted SFML code provides a clear interface for others to understand and use. Team members can focus on different aspects of the project without needing an in-depth understanding of the entire codebase.

4. **Testing:** Abstraction simplifies the testing process. You can create unit tests for individual components, ensuring that they work correctly in isolation before integrating them into the larger application.

Creating an SFML Abstraction Layer

To abstract SFML for modular development, you can follow these steps:

1. **Identify Components:** Identify the SFML components and functionality that you want to abstract. These may include graphics rendering, audio playback, input handling, and more.

2. **Create Abstraction Classes or Modules:** Design classes or modules that encapsulate SFML functionality. For example, you can create a GraphicsModule class that handles rendering, textures, and sprites.

3. **Define Interfaces:** Define clear and consistent interfaces for your abstraction classes. This includes defining functions, methods, and data structures that provide a high-level way to interact with SFML features.

4. **Encapsulate SFML Details:** Within your abstraction classes, encapsulate the low-level SFML details. This shields the rest of your application from the intricacies of SFML's API.

5. **Test Abstraction:** Write tests to ensure that your abstraction layer works as expected. These tests should verify that the abstraction correctly translates high-level commands into SFML actions.

Code Example: Abstracting Keyboard Input

Let's consider a simple example of abstracting keyboard input with SFML. We'll create an InputManager class that encapsulates SFML's keyboard handling.

```cpp
#include <SFML/Graphics.hpp>

class InputManager {
public:
    bool isKeyPressed(sf::Keyboard::Key key) {
        return sf::Keyboard::isKeyPressed(key);
    }
};

int main() {
    sf::RenderWindow window(sf::VideoMode(800, 600), "Abstracting SFML Input"
);

    InputManager inputManager;

    while (window.isOpen()) {
        sf::Event event;
        while (window.pollEvent(event)) {
            if (event.type == sf::Event::Closed) {
                window.close();
            }
        }

        // Check for keyboard input using the abstraction
        if (inputManager.isKeyPressed(sf::Keyboard::Space)) {
            // Handle Space key press
        }
```

```
        window.clear();
        // Draw your application content here
        window.display();
    }

    return 0;
}
```

In this example, the `InputManager` class provides a higher-level interface for checking if a specific key is pressed. This abstraction simplifies the handling of keyboard input in your application and can be reused throughout your project.

Abstracting SFML for modular development is a valuable practice, especially in large-scale projects or when working collaboratively. It promotes code reusability, maintainability, and easier testing while allowing developers to focus on high-level application logic rather than low-level SFML details.

Chapter 2: Advanced Graphics Rendering with SFML

Section 2.1: Implementing Custom Shaders for Graphics

In this section, we will dive deep into the world of custom shaders for graphics rendering with SFML. Shaders are powerful tools that allow you to manipulate the appearance of graphics in real-time, creating stunning visual effects and enhancing the realism of your applications. Understanding how to implement custom shaders is essential for taking your graphics rendering to the next level.

The Power of Shaders

Shaders are small programs written in languages like GLSL (OpenGL Shading Language) or HLSL (High-Level Shading Language) that run on the GPU (Graphics Processing Unit). They are used to control various aspects of graphics rendering, including colors, lighting, textures, and more. Here are some key reasons why shaders are invaluable:

1. **Real-Time Rendering:** Shaders enable real-time rendering of complex effects that would be computationally expensive to achieve using traditional CPU-based techniques.

2. **Customization:** With shaders, you have complete control over the rendering pipeline, allowing you to create custom effects tailored to your application's needs.

3. **Visual Appeal:** Shaders can significantly enhance the visual appeal of your applications by adding effects like dynamic lighting, post-processing filters, and realistic materials.

4. **Efficiency:** GPU parallelism makes shaders highly efficient for tasks like rendering complex scenes, making them essential for modern graphics applications.

Shader Types in SFML

SFML supports two main types of shaders: vertex shaders and fragment shaders. Vertex shaders manipulate the position and attributes of vertices, while fragment shaders control the final color of each pixel. Together, they allow for a wide range of graphical effects.

To implement custom shaders in SFML, you'll typically follow these steps:

1. **Load Shader Programs:** Load shader programs from external files or strings in your application.

2. **Attach Shaders:** Attach vertex and fragment shaders to an `sf::Shader` object.

3. **Set Shader Parameters:** Set shader parameters, such as uniforms, to control the behavior of the shader.

4. **Apply the Shader:** Apply the shader to the rendering process using `sf::RenderWindow::draw()`.

Code Example: Implementing a Simple Shader

Let's look at a basic example of implementing a custom shader in SFML. In this example, we'll create a simple vertex shader that displaces vertices based on time, creating a waving effect.

```cpp
#include <SFML/Graphics.hpp>

const char* vertexShader = R"(
    void main() {
        gl_Position = gl_ModelViewProjectionMatrix * gl_Vertex;
        gl_Position.y += 0.1 * sin(gl_Vertex.x + gl_Vertex.y + gl_Vertex.z +
gl_SecondaryColor.x);
    }
)";

int main() {
    sf::RenderWindow window(sf::VideoMode(800, 600), "Custom Shader Example")
;

    sf::Shader shader;
    shader.loadFromMemory(vertexShader, sf::Shader::Vertex);

    while (window.isOpen()) {
        sf::Event event;
        while (window.pollEvent(event)) {
            if (event.type == sf::Event::Closed) {
                window.close();
            }
        }

        window.clear();
        // Apply the shader to the rendering process
        window.draw(sf::RectangleShape(sf::Vector2f(400, 400)), &shader);
        window.display();
    }

    return 0;
}
```

In this code, we create a simple vertex shader that displaces vertices along the Y-axis based on time and the vertex's position. The shader is then applied to a rectangle drawn in the window, creating a waving effect.

Understanding and implementing custom shaders opens up a world of possibilities for advanced graphics rendering in SFML. In the upcoming sections of this chapter, we will explore more complex shader techniques, including fragment shaders and post-processing effects, to create visually stunning graphics for your applications.

Section 2.2: Using OpenGL with SFML for High-Performance Rendering

In this section, we will explore the integration of OpenGL with SFML to achieve high-performance graphics rendering. While SFML provides a user-friendly and cross-platform interface for graphics, OpenGL offers low-level access to the GPU, allowing for advanced rendering techniques and optimal performance. Combining the power of both libraries can be highly advantageous for applications that require top-notch graphics performance.

The Role of OpenGL

OpenGL (Open Graphics Library) is an open-standard graphics API that provides direct access to the GPU. It allows developers to harness the full power of modern graphics hardware, making it a popular choice for applications demanding high-performance graphics. Here are some reasons to consider using OpenGL with SFML:

1. **Hardware Acceleration:** OpenGL leverages GPU acceleration, resulting in significantly faster rendering compared to CPU-based graphics rendering.

2. **Advanced Techniques:** With OpenGL, you have access to a wide range of advanced graphics techniques, including custom shaders, 3D rendering, and post-processing effects.

3. **Cross-Platform:** Like SFML, OpenGL is cross-platform and supported on various operating systems, making it a versatile choice for multi-platform development.

4. **Low-Level Control:** OpenGL provides low-level control over the rendering pipeline, making it suitable for fine-tuning graphics performance.

Integrating OpenGL with SFML

SFML makes it relatively straightforward to integrate OpenGL into your applications. Here are the general steps to follow:

1. **Create an OpenGL Window:** Use SFML to create an OpenGL rendering context. This is done by setting the appropriate attributes when creating an `sf::RenderWindow` or `sf::Window`.

2. **Initialize OpenGL:** Use GLEW (OpenGL Extension Wrangler Library) or a similar library to load OpenGL extensions and functions. This ensures that you can access the full set of OpenGL features.

3. **Use OpenGL Functions:** Once initialized, you can use OpenGL functions to perform rendering tasks. This includes setting up vertex and fragment shaders, working with vertex buffers, and performing advanced rendering operations.

4. **Combine SFML and OpenGL:** You can use SFML for tasks like window management, input handling, and texture loading while utilizing OpenGL for rendering tasks. SFML provides the `sf::Texture::getNativeHandle()` function to get the OpenGL texture handle for SFML textures, facilitating seamless integration.

Code Example: Creating an OpenGL Window

Here's a simple example of creating an OpenGL window using SFML:

```cpp
#include <SFML/Graphics.hpp>
#include <SFML/OpenGL.hpp>

int main() {
    sf::RenderWindow window(sf::VideoMode(800, 600), "OpenGL with SFML", sf::
Style::Default, sf::ContextSettings(32)); // Create an OpenGL context with 32
bits of depth
    window.setVerticalSyncEnabled(true); // Enable vertical synchronization

    // Initialize OpenGL (GLEW or similar library is required)
    if (glewInit() != GLEW_OK) {
        return 1; // Error handling for OpenGL initialization
    }

    // OpenGL rendering loop
    while (window.isOpen()) {
        sf::Event event;
        while (window.pollEvent(event)) {
            if (event.type == sf::Event::Closed) {
                window.close();
            }
        }

        // OpenGL rendering code here

        window.display();
    }

    return 0;
}
```

In this code, we create an OpenGL context within an SFML window. The `sf::ContextSettings(32)` ensures a 32-bit depth buffer for 3D rendering. You can then use OpenGL functions for advanced rendering within the SFML window.

Using OpenGL with SFML provides a powerful combination of high-performance graphics and a user-friendly interface. In the upcoming sections of this chapter, we will explore more advanced graphics techniques with OpenGL integration, including custom shaders and 3D graphics rendering.

Section 2.3: Advanced 2D Graphics Techniques

In this section, we will explore advanced 2D graphics techniques using SFML. While SFML is known for its simplicity, it also provides the tools necessary to create visually stunning 2D graphics for your applications and games. Understanding these advanced techniques will enable you to push the boundaries of what you can achieve with 2D graphics.

Optimized Sprite Rendering

SFML's `sf::Sprite` class makes it easy to display textures, but for performance-critical applications or games, optimizing sprite rendering is essential. Here are some techniques for optimized sprite rendering:

1. **Sprite Batching:** Group similar sprites together and draw them in a single batch. This reduces the number of draw calls, improving performance.

2. **Texture Atlases:** Combine multiple textures into a single texture atlas. This minimizes texture binding and improves rendering speed.

3. **Vertex Arrays:** Use `sf::VertexArray` to draw sprites in bulk. This allows you to specify vertices and texture coordinates directly for improved performance.

Particle Systems

Particle systems are essential for creating dynamic and immersive visual effects. SFML provides the flexibility to implement custom particle systems. Key components of a particle system include:

1. **Particle Representation:** Define the visual properties of each particle, such as position, velocity, size, and color.

2. **Emitter:** Create an emitter that generates particles over time. You can control the emission rate, direction, and initial properties of particles.

3. **Particle Update:** Implement logic to update particle positions and properties over time. This may involve physics simulations, such as gravity and collisions.

4. **Rendering:** Draw particles using optimized rendering techniques to minimize performance overhead.

Dynamic Lighting

Creating dynamic lighting effects can greatly enhance the visual appeal of your 2D graphics. To implement dynamic lighting in SFML:

1. **Shader-Based Lighting:** Use custom shaders to simulate lighting effects, such as shadows, highlights, and ambient lighting. Shaders allow for real-time calculations of lighting interactions.

2. **Light Sources:** Define light sources in your scene, each with a position, intensity, and color. Calculate the influence of each light source on nearby objects using shaders.

3. **Textures for Lighting:** Create textures that represent lighting information. These textures can be updated in real-time to reflect changes in the scene's lighting conditions.

Layered Rendering

Layered rendering involves dividing your scene into layers, each containing specific elements. This technique allows for more control over rendering order and can improve efficiency. Common layers include:

1. **Background Layer:** Contains static or slow-moving elements, such as the background of a game level.

2. **Foreground Layer:** Contains objects that need to be rendered in front of other elements, such as characters and interactive objects.

3. **UI Layer:** Holds user interface elements like menus, health bars, and text.

By organizing your scene into layers, you can optimize rendering by reducing the need for complex sorting algorithms and controlling the rendering order more effectively.

Code Example: Optimized Sprite Rendering

Here's a code example demonstrating optimized sprite rendering using sprite batching with SFML:

```cpp
#include <SFML/Graphics.hpp>

int main() {
    sf::RenderWindow window(sf::VideoMode(800, 600), "Optimized Sprite Rendering");

    sf::Texture texture;
    if (!texture.loadFromFile("sprite.png")) {
        return 1; // Handle texture loading error
    }

    // Create a sprite batch
    std::vector<sf::Sprite> spriteBatch;

    // Populate the sprite batch
    for (int i = 0; i < 1000; ++i) {
        sf::Sprite sprite(texture);
        sprite.setPosition(i * 20, i * 20); // Adjust positions as needed
        spriteBatch.push_back(sprite);
    }
```

```
while (window.isOpen()) {
    sf::Event event;
    while (window.pollEvent(event)) {
        if (event.type == sf::Event::Closed) {
            window.close();
        }
    }

    window.clear();

    // Draw the entire sprite batch in a single draw call
    for (const sf::Sprite& sprite : spriteBatch) {
        window.draw(sprite);
    }

    window.display();
}

return 0;
}
```

In this example, we create a sprite batch by storing `sf::Sprite` objects in a vector. By drawing all sprites in a single loop, we optimize sprite rendering by minimizing the number of draw calls.

Advanced 2D graphics techniques in SFML allow you to create visually appealing and performance-efficient applications and games. Whether it's optimizing sprite rendering, implementing particle systems, adding dynamic lighting, or organizing layered rendering, mastering these techniques can significantly enhance the quality of your 2D graphics.

Section 2.4: Implementing Post-Processing Effects

In this section, we will delve into the fascinating world of post-processing effects in SFML. Post-processing effects are visual enhancements applied to the entire rendered scene after all objects have been drawn. They can dramatically alter the appearance of your graphics, adding realism, style, and immersion to your applications and games.

What Are Post-Processing Effects?

Post-processing effects, often referred to as shaders or filters, are graphical algorithms applied to the final rendered image. They modify the colors, lighting, and visual characteristics of the scene to achieve various artistic or realistic effects. Some common post-processing effects include:

1. **Bloom:** Enhances bright areas of the image, creating a glowing or ethereal look.

2. **Blur:** Blurs the entire image or specific regions, simulating depth of field or motion.

3. **Grayscale:** Converts the image to grayscale for a classic or dramatic effect.

4. **Sepia Tone:** Gives the image a warm, nostalgic appearance.

5. **Distortion:** Warps the image to simulate underwater effects, heatwaves, or other distortions.

6. **HDR (High Dynamic Range):** Enhances the contrast and color range of the image for a more vivid look.

Implementing Post-Processing Effects in SFML

SFML makes it relatively straightforward to implement post-processing effects using custom shaders. Here's a general overview of how to apply post-processing effects:

1. **Create Shader Programs:** Write shader programs in GLSL or HLSL that define the desired post-processing effect. These shaders will be responsible for modifying the final image.

2. **Load Shaders:** Load the shader programs into an `sf::Shader` object.

3. **Render to Texture:** Instead of rendering directly to the window, render the scene to an off-screen texture.

4. **Apply Shader:** Apply the shader to the off-screen texture, which contains the rendered scene. This applies the post-processing effect to the entire scene.

5. **Draw Final Image:** Finally, draw the off-screen texture (now modified by the shader) to the window.

Code Example: Implementing a Simple Post-Processing Effect

Let's explore a simple example of implementing a grayscale post-processing effect in SFML:

```cpp
#include <SFML/Graphics.hpp>

const char* fragmentShader = R"(
    uniform sampler2D texture;
    void main() {
        vec4 color = texture2D(texture, gl_TexCoord[0].xy);
        float gray = dot(color.rgb, vec3(0.299, 0.587, 0.114));
        gl_FragColor = vec4(vec3(gray), color.a);
    }
)";

int main() {
    sf::RenderWindow window(sf::VideoMode(800, 600), "Grayscale Effect Exampl
e");
```

```
sf::Shader shader;
shader.loadFromMemory(fragmentShader, sf::Shader::Fragment);

sf::RenderTexture renderTexture;
renderTexture.create(800, 600);

while (window.isOpen()) {
    sf::Event event;
    while (window.pollEvent(event)) {
        if (event.type == sf::Event::Closed) {
            window.close();
        }
    }

    // Draw your scene to the off-screen texture
    renderTexture.clear();
    renderTexture.draw(/* your scene here */);
    renderTexture.display();

    // Apply the shader to the off-screen texture
    shader.setUniform("texture", renderTexture.getTexture());

    window.clear();

    // Draw the modified texture with the shader applied
    sf::Sprite sprite(renderTexture.getTexture());
    window.draw(sprite, &shader);

    window.display();
}

    return 0;
}
```

In this code, we create a simple grayscale effect by applying a custom fragment shader. The scene is first rendered to an off-screen texture, and then the shader is applied to that texture. Finally, we draw the modified texture to the window, achieving the grayscale effect.

Post-processing effects offer a creative way to enhance your graphics and create visually engaging applications and games. By exploring and experimenting with custom shaders, you can achieve a wide range of effects, from subtle enhancements to dramatic transformations of your rendered scenes.

Section 2.5: Integrating 3D Graphics Elements with SFML

In this section, we'll explore how to integrate 3D graphics elements with SFML. While SFML is primarily a 2D graphics library, it's possible to incorporate 3D elements into your applications for added depth and complexity. This can be particularly useful when building games or simulations that require both 2D and 3D components.

The 2D/3D Integration Challenge

SFML is designed primarily for 2D graphics, so integrating 3D elements involves some additional considerations. To integrate 3D graphics effectively, you can follow these steps:

1. **Use OpenGL:** While SFML provides a simplified interface for 2D graphics, it's beneficial to have a good understanding of OpenGL for 3D rendering. OpenGL allows you to create and manipulate 3D objects efficiently.

2. **Create an OpenGL Context:** When initializing your SFML application, ensure you create an OpenGL context. This is necessary for rendering 3D graphics with OpenGL.

3. **Combine SFML and OpenGL:** You can use SFML for window management, input handling, and 2D graphics rendering. For 3D rendering, use OpenGL functions to create and manipulate 3D objects, textures, and shaders.

4. **Coordinate Systems:** Be aware of the differences in coordinate systems between SFML and OpenGL. SFML uses a 2D Cartesian coordinate system, while OpenGL typically uses a 3D coordinate system with depth.

5. **Camera Setup:** Implement a camera system to control the view and perspective of your 3D scene. This allows you to navigate and interact with the 3D environment.

Integrating 3D Models

To integrate 3D models into your SFML application, you'll need to consider the following:

1. **Model Loading:** Use libraries like Assimp to load 3D models in common formats (e.g., OBJ, FBX). These libraries provide functions to parse and import 3D models.

2. **Shader Setup:** Create custom shaders to render 3D models with realistic lighting, materials, and textures. OpenGL shaders play a crucial role in 3D rendering.

3. **Transformations:** Implement transformations such as translation, rotation, and scaling to position and animate 3D models within the 3D space.

4. **Rendering Loop:** Integrate the 3D rendering within your main rendering loop alongside SFML's 2D rendering. This ensures that both 2D and 3D elements are drawn correctly.

Code Example: Integrating a 3D Cube

Here's a simple example of how to integrate a 3D cube into an SFML application using OpenGL:

```cpp
#include <SFML/Graphics.hpp>
#include <SFML/OpenGL.hpp>

int main() {
    sf::RenderWindow window(sf::VideoMode(800, 600), "3D Cube Example");
    window.setVerticalSyncEnabled(true);

    // Create an OpenGL context
    sf::ContextSettings settings;
    settings.depthBits = 24;
    window.create(sf::VideoMode(800, 600), "3D Cube Example", sf::Style::Defa
ult, settings);

    // Set up a simple OpenGL projection
    glViewport(0, 0, 800, 600);
    glMatrixMode(GL_PROJECTION);
    glLoadIdentity();
    gluPerspective(90.f, 800.f / 600.f, 1.f, 500.f);

    while (window.isOpen()) {
        sf::Event event;
        while (window.pollEvent(event)) {
            if (event.type == sf::Event::Closed) {
                window.close();
            }
        }

        // Clear the depth buffer
        glClear(GL_COLOR_BUFFER_BIT | GL_DEPTH_BUFFER_BIT);

        // 3D rendering code here (e.g., drawing a cube)

        window.display();
    }

    return 0;
}
```

In this example, we create an OpenGL context within the SFML window and set up a simple perspective projection for 3D rendering. While the example does not include drawing a 3D cube, you can add OpenGL commands to render 3D objects within the rendering loop.

Integrating 3D graphics with SFML opens up exciting possibilities for creating immersive applications and games. With a solid understanding of OpenGL and the integration techniques mentioned above, you can incorporate 3D elements seamlessly alongside SFML's 2D graphics, enhancing the overall visual experience of your projects.

Chapter 3: Building Cross-Platform Applications

Section 3.1: Cross-Platform Development Strategies

In this section, we will explore cross-platform development strategies and best practices when building applications with SFML. Cross-platform development involves creating software that can run on multiple operating systems with minimal code modifications. SFML's cross-platform capabilities make it an excellent choice for developing applications that target various platforms, including Windows, macOS, Linux, iOS, and Android.

Why Cross-Platform Development Matters

Cross-platform development offers several advantages:

1. **Wider Reach:** By targeting multiple platforms, you can reach a broader audience, including users on different devices and operating systems.

2. **Cost Efficiency:** Developing for multiple platforms simultaneously can be more cost-effective than creating separate applications for each.

3. **Consistency:** Cross-platform development ensures a consistent user experience across different devices and platforms.

4. **Maintenance:** Maintaining a single codebase for multiple platforms simplifies updates and bug fixes.

Key Strategies for Cross-Platform Development

When developing cross-platform applications with SFML, consider the following strategies:

1. **Platform Abstraction:** Use SFML's platform-independent features and abstractions to minimize platform-specific code. For example, use SFML's file and network APIs instead of writing platform-specific code for file I/O or network communication.

2. **Conditional Compilation:** Use preprocessor directives and conditional compilation to include or exclude platform-specific code sections. For example, you can use `#ifdef _WIN32` to conditionally compile code for Windows.

3. **Testing on Target Platforms:** Regularly test your application on all target platforms to identify and resolve platform-specific issues early in the development process.

4. **Version Control:** Use version control systems like Git to manage your codebase efficiently. Branching can be helpful for maintaining platform-specific code branches.

5. **Cross-Platform Libraries:** Consider using cross-platform libraries or frameworks that provide consistent APIs across different platforms. SFML itself is cross-platform, but you may need additional libraries for specific functionality.

6. **Responsive Design:** Design your user interface and user experience to be responsive and adaptable to different screen sizes and resolutions. SFML provides tools for managing various window sizes and aspect ratios.

Code Example: Platform-Independent File I/O

Here's an example of how to perform platform-independent file I/O with SFML:

```cpp
#include <SFML/System.hpp>

int main() {
    // Platform-independent file loading
    sf::FileInputStream file;
    if (file.open("data.txt")) {
        // Read data from the file
        // ...
        file.close();
    } else {
        // Handle file not found or other errors
        // ...
    }

    return 0;
}
```

In this code, we use `sf::FileInputStream` for file I/O, which abstracts platform-specific file operations. The same code can be used on Windows, macOS, and Linux without modification.

Cross-platform development is essential for reaching a diverse user base and ensuring your application's success on different devices and operating systems. By following best practices, leveraging SFML's cross-platform features, and testing on target platforms, you can create robust and versatile applications that work seamlessly across various environments.

Section 3.2: Targeting iOS with SFML

In this section, we will explore the process of targeting iOS, Apple's mobile operating system, with applications developed using SFML. iOS is a popular platform for mobile app development, and while SFML is primarily known for desktop applications, it is possible to create iOS apps with SFML by leveraging the right tools and techniques.

Before you begin developing iOS apps with SFML, you need to set up your development environment and acquire the necessary tools. Here are some prerequisites:

1. **Xcode:** Xcode is Apple's integrated development environment (IDE) for iOS app development. You'll need to install Xcode from the Mac App Store.

2. **macOS:** You need a Mac computer to develop and build iOS apps due to Apple's development restrictions.

3. **SFML for iOS:** You'll need a version of SFML compiled for iOS. You can either build it from source using the iOS-specific CMake files provided with SFML or use precompiled libraries.

4. **Apple Developer Account:** To deploy and test apps on iOS devices or distribute them through the App Store, you'll need an Apple Developer Account.

Building and Running an SFML iOS App

Here's a high-level overview of the steps to build and run an SFML-based iOS app:

1. **Create an SFML iOS Project:** Set up a new Xcode project for iOS development and configure it to use SFML. You'll need to link the SFML libraries and set up the necessary build settings.

2. **Code Your App:** Write your application code using the SFML API. You can create iOS-specific code for things like touch input handling.

3. **Deployment Target:** Set the deployment target in Xcode to the iOS version you want to support (e.g., iOS 12.0).

4. **Testing on Simulator:** You can test your app on the iOS Simulator provided by Xcode. This allows you to see how your app behaves on different iOS devices.

5. **Provisioning Profiles:** Set up provisioning profiles for your app in the Apple Developer Portal. These profiles are required to run your app on physical iOS devices.

6. **Code Signing:** Configure code signing settings in Xcode using your Apple Developer Account credentials.

7. **Testing on Physical Devices:** Connect your iOS device to your Mac and select it as the target device in Xcode. You can now test your app on a real iOS device.

8. **Distribution:** If you want to distribute your app on the App Store or share it with others, follow Apple's guidelines for app distribution.

Code Example: SFML iOS App Initialization

Here's a simplified code example showing how to initialize an SFML-based iOS app:

```cpp
#include <SFML/Graphics.hpp>

int main(int argc, char** argv) {
    sf::RenderWindow window(sf::VideoMode(800, 600), "SFML iOS App");

    while (window.isOpen()) {
        sf::Event event;
        while (window.pollEvent(event)) {
            if (event.type == sf::Event::Closed) {
                window.close();
            }
        }

        window.clear(sf::Color::White);
        // Your SFML drawing and logic here
        window.display();
    }

    return 0;
}
```

This code sets up an SFML window and a simple event loop. You can extend this code to create your iOS app with SFML.

Targeting iOS with SFML allows you to bring your SFML-based applications to a mobile audience. While the process involves additional steps and considerations compared to desktop development, it opens up opportunities to reach iOS users with your SFML-powered applications.

Section 3.3: Building Android Apps with SFML

In this section, we will explore the process of building Android applications using SFML, allowing you to target the Android platform with your SFML-based projects. Android is one of the most widely used mobile operating systems, and by leveraging SFML, you can create cross-platform applications that work on both desktop and Android devices.

Prerequisites for Android Development with SFML

Before you start building Android apps with SFML, you need to set up your development environment and obtain the necessary tools. Here are some prerequisites:

1. **Android Studio:** Android Studio is the official integrated development environment (IDE) for Android app development. You'll need to download and install it.

2. **Java Development Kit (JDK):** Android app development is primarily done using Java. Install the appropriate version of the JDK.

3. **SFML for Android:** You'll need a version of SFML that's compiled for Android. You can either build it from source using the Android-specific CMake files provided with SFML or use precompiled libraries.

4. **Android NDK:** The Android Native Development Kit (NDK) allows you to write native code for Android. You may need it if you plan to use certain SFML features or integrate third-party libraries.

5. **Android Device or Emulator:** You can test your Android app on a physical Android device or an emulator provided by Android Studio.

6. **Google Play Developer Account:** To distribute your app on the Google Play Store, you'll need a Google Play Developer Account.

Building and Running an SFML Android App

Here's an overview of the steps to build and run an SFML-based Android app:

1. **Create an SFML Android Project:** Set up a new Android project in Android Studio and configure it to use SFML. This involves linking the SFML libraries and setting up build settings.

2. **Coding Your App:** Write the application code using the SFML API. You may need to add Android-specific code for permissions, device features, and handling touch input.

3. **Testing on Emulator:** Use the Android Emulator provided by Android Studio to test your app on virtual Android devices with different screen sizes and configurations.

4. **Testing on Physical Devices:** Connect an Android device to your computer and enable USB debugging. You can then deploy and test your app directly on the device.

5. **APK Generation:** Generate an Android Package (APK) file for your app, which is the installation package for Android apps.

6. **Signing the APK:** Sign your APK with a keystore to ensure it can be installed on Android devices.

7. **Deployment:** You can distribute your app through various channels, including the Google Play Store, other Android app stores, or direct distribution.

Code Example: SFML Android App Initialization

Here's a simplified code example demonstrating how to initialize an SFML-based Android app:

```cpp
#include <SFML/Graphics.hpp>

int main() {
    sf::RenderWindow window(sf::VideoMode(800, 600), "SFML Android App");
```

```
    while (window.isOpen()) {
        sf::Event event;
        while (window.pollEvent(event)) {
            if (event.type == sf::Event::Closed) {
                window.close();
            }
        }

        window.clear(sf::Color::White);
        // Your SFML drawing and logic here
        window.display();
    }

    return 0;
}
```

This code sets up an SFML window and a simple event loop, similar to the desktop example. You can expand upon this code to create your Android app with SFML.

Building Android apps with SFML extends the reach of your applications to a wide range of Android devices. While the Android development process has its intricacies, SFML's flexibility allows you to create cross-platform apps that run smoothly on both desktop and Android environments, enhancing the accessibility of your projects.

Section 3.4: Ensuring Compatibility Across Multiple Platforms

In this section, we will explore strategies for ensuring compatibility across multiple platforms when developing applications with SFML. Cross-platform development involves addressing the differences in hardware, operating systems, and configurations among your target platforms. Ensuring compatibility is crucial for providing a consistent user experience across various devices and environments.

Challenges in Cross-Platform Compatibility

Cross-platform development introduces several challenges, including:

1. **Diverse Hardware:** Different platforms have varying hardware capabilities, such as CPU power, memory, and graphics capabilities. Your application should gracefully handle these differences.

2. **Operating System Variations:** Each operating system may have unique behaviors, APIs, and system limitations. Adapting your code to work seamlessly on each OS is essential.

3. **Screen Resolutions:** Devices come in various screen sizes and resolutions. Your user interface and graphics should scale and adapt accordingly.

4. **Input Methods:** Users interact with devices differently, whether it's through touchscreens, keyboards, mice, or game controllers. Your application should support multiple input methods.

To ensure compatibility across multiple platforms when using SFML, consider the following strategies:

1. **Feature Detection:** Detect and check for specific hardware or software features at runtime. For example, check if a device supports multitouch input before enabling related features.

2. **Responsive Design:** Design your user interface to be responsive and adaptable to different screen sizes and resolutions. Use SFML's view and viewport features to manage varying aspect ratios.

3. **Modular Code:** Organize your codebase into modular components, making it easier to implement platform-specific code or features without affecting the entire project.

4. **Platform Abstraction:** Use SFML's platform-independent features and abstractions as much as possible. Avoid relying on platform-specific APIs unless necessary.

5. **Conditional Compilation:** Use preprocessor directives and conditional compilation to include or exclude platform-specific code sections. For example, use #ifdef _WIN32 for Windows-specific code.

6. **Testing on Target Platforms:** Regularly test your application on all target platforms to identify and resolve platform-specific issues early in development.

7. **User Feedback:** Encourage user feedback to identify and address compatibility issues on different platforms. Users can provide valuable insights into problems they encounter.

8. **Version Control:** Use version control systems like Git to manage your codebase efficiently, especially when dealing with platform-specific code branches.

Here's a simplified code example demonstrating feature detection for multitouch support using SFML:

```cpp
#include <SFML/Graphics.hpp>

int main() {
    sf::RenderWindow window(sf::VideoMode(800, 600), "Cross-Platform Compatibility Example");

    // Check if the device supports multitouch input
    bool supportsMultitouch = sf::Touch::isSupported();
```

```
while (window.isOpen()) {
    sf::Event event;
    while (window.pollEvent(event)) {
        if (event.type == sf::Event::Closed) {
            window.close();
        }

        // Handle multitouch input only if supported
        if (supportsMultitouch && event.type == sf::Event::TouchBegan) {
            // Handle multitouch input here
        }
    }

    window.clear(sf::Color::White);
    // Your SFML drawing and logic here
    window.display();
}

return 0;
}
```

In this code, we check if the device supports multitouch input using `sf::Touch::isSupported()`. If supported, we handle multitouch input events. This feature detection ensures that we only use multitouch functionality on devices where it's available.

Cross-platform compatibility is essential for providing a seamless user experience across various devices and operating systems. By following these strategies and considering the unique characteristics of each target platform, you can develop applications with SFML that work reliably on desktop, mobile, and other platforms.

Section 3.5: Handling Platform-Specific Features and Considerations

In this section, we will discuss how to handle platform-specific features and considerations when developing cross-platform applications with SFML. While SFML provides a unified API for many tasks, there are cases where you may need to implement platform-specific functionality or adapt your code to meet platform-specific requirements.

Identifying Platform-Specific Needs

Before addressing platform-specific features, it's crucial to identify what aspects of your application require platform-specific attention. Here are some common areas:

1. **Input Methods:** Different platforms may have distinct input methods or devices. For example, handling touch input on mobile devices differs from keyboard and mouse input on desktop.

2. **File Paths:** File path conventions can vary between operating systems (e.g., using backslashes \ on Windows and forward slashes / on Unix-based systems). You may need to handle path conversion.

3. **Window Management:** Window creation, resizing, and fullscreen modes may have platform-specific considerations.

4. **File I/O:** File I/O operations can behave differently on various platforms, especially concerning file permissions.

5. **System Libraries:** Accessing platform-specific system libraries or APIs may be necessary for certain features.

Platform-Specific Code Sections

To address platform-specific needs in your SFML application, you can use conditional compilation and platform-specific code sections. Here's an example of platform-specific code for handling window events:

```cpp
#include <SFML/Graphics.hpp>

int main() {
    sf::RenderWindow window(sf::VideoMode(800, 600), "Cross-Platform App");

#ifdef _WIN32
    // Windows-specific code
    window.setFramerateLimit(60);
#elif __APPLE__
    // macOS-specific code
    window.setVerticalSyncEnabled(true);
#else
    // Default behavior for other platforms
#endif

    while (window.isOpen()) {
        sf::Event event;
        while (window.pollEvent(event)) {
            if (event.type == sf::Event::Closed) {
                window.close();
            }
        }

        window.clear(sf::Color::White);
        // Your SFML drawing and logic here
        window.display();
    }

    return 0;
}
```

In this code, we use preprocessor directives (#ifdef, #elif, #else) to conditionally compile code based on the target platform. This allows you to apply different settings and behaviors on different platforms while maintaining a single codebase.

Handling Path Conversions

Dealing with file paths in a cross-platform application can be challenging due to differences in path conventions. To handle this, you can use SFML's sf::String and sf::String::fromUtf8 functions to convert between different string encodings. Here's an example of converting a path to UTF-8:

```cpp
#include <SFML/System.hpp>
#include <iostream>

int main() {
    std::string path = "C:\\Users\\User\\Documents\\file.txt";

#ifdef _WIN32
    // Convert path to UTF-8 for Windows
    sf::String utf8Path = sf::String::fromUtf8(path.begin(), path.end());
    std::cout << "UTF-8 Path: " << utf8Path.toUtf8() << std::endl;
#else
    // Use the original path for other platforms
    std::cout << "Path: " << path << std::endl;
#endif

    return 0;
}
```

In this code, we convert the file path to UTF-8 format for Windows, ensuring compatibility with SFML's file operations.

Platform-Specific Libraries and APIs

For cases where you need to access platform-specific libraries or APIs, you can use external libraries or write native code using the Android NDK (for Android) or Objective-C/C++ (for iOS and macOS). These libraries or native code can be integrated with your SFML-based application as needed.

Handling platform-specific features and considerations is an integral part of cross-platform development with SFML. By identifying and addressing these aspects, you can create applications that provide a consistent and optimized user experience on different platforms while maximizing code reusability.

Chapter 4: Designing a Multimedia Player

Section 4.1: Creating a Multimedia Player Project

In this section, we'll delve into the process of creating a multimedia player project using SFML. Multimedia players are applications that can play various types of media, such as audio and video files. By the end of this chapter, you'll have a functional multimedia player that leverages SFML's capabilities for multimedia playback.

Understanding the Requirements

Before diving into the implementation, it's crucial to understand the requirements of a multimedia player project. These requirements may include:

1. **File Format Support:** Determine which audio and video formats your player should support. SFML provides support for common formats like MP3, WAV, and OGG for audio, but you may need additional libraries or plugins for other formats.

2. **User Interface:** Design a user-friendly interface for your player, including features like play, pause, stop, volume control, and progress tracking.

3. **Playback Control:** Implement controls for starting, pausing, stopping, and seeking through media files. You'll also need features like repeat and shuffle.

4. **Playlist Management:** Allow users to create and manage playlists for their media files.

5. **Audio Visualization:** Consider implementing audio visualization features, such as spectrum analyzers or visualizers that respond to the audio being played.

6. **Cross-Platform Compatibility:** Ensure that your player works seamlessly on different operating systems.

Setting Up the Project

To start the multimedia player project, you can create a new C++ project using an IDE or build system of your choice. Here are the initial steps:

1. **Include SFML:** Make sure you have SFML properly installed and set up in your project. You'll need the audio and window modules for the multimedia player.

2. **User Interface:** Choose a user interface framework or library for building the player's interface. SFML itself focuses on low-level graphics, so you may want to use an additional library like ImGui or Qt for creating the user interface.

3. **Audio and Video Codecs:** If your player needs to support various media formats, you may need to incorporate third-party libraries or codecs. Libraries like FFmpeg or GStreamer can help with decoding and encoding different media types.

Here's a basic code example to initialize SFML and create a window for your multimedia player project:

```
#include <SFML/Graphics.hpp>

int main() {
    sf::RenderWindow window(sf::VideoMode(800, 600), "Multimedia Player");

    while (window.isOpen()) {
        sf::Event event;
        while (window.pollEvent(event)) {
            if (event.type == sf::Event::Closed) {
                window.close();
            }
        }

        window.clear(sf::Color::Black);
        // Your multimedia player UI and logic here
        window.display();
    }

    return 0;
}
```

This code initializes SFML, creates a window, and sets up a basic event loop. You can build upon this foundation to create the user interface and implement multimedia playback functionalities in your project.

Designing a multimedia player with SFML offers flexibility and control over various aspects of media playback and user interaction. By carefully defining your project's requirements and setting up the initial project structure, you can embark on the development journey with a clear direction toward creating a feature-rich multimedia player.

Section 4.2: Handling Audio and Video Playback

In this section, we will explore how to handle audio and video playback in a multimedia player project using SFML. Playing audio and video files is a core functionality of multimedia players, and SFML provides the necessary tools and features to achieve this.

Audio Playback with SFML

SFML's audio module allows you to play various audio formats, making it suitable for audio playback in your multimedia player. To play audio, you'll need to follow these steps:

1. **Include the Appropriate Headers:** Include the necessary SFML audio headers in your project.

```cpp
#include <SFML/Audio.hpp>
```

2. **Load Audio Files:** Load the audio files you want to play into SFML's `sf::SoundBuffer` objects.

```cpp
sf::SoundBuffer buffer;
if (!buffer.loadFromFile("audio_file.wav")) {
    // Handle loading error
}
```

3. **Create Sound Objects:** Create instances of `sf::Sound` to represent the audio and set their respective buffers.

```cpp
sf::Sound sound;
sound.setBuffer(buffer);
```

4. **Playback Control:** You can control the playback of audio by using methods like `play()`, `pause()`, `stop()`, and adjusting the volume with `setVolume()`.

```cpp
sound.play(); // Start playback
sound.pause(); // Pause playback
sound.stop(); // Stop playback
sound.setVolume(50); // Set volume (0-100)
```

5. **Handling Events:** Implement event handling to respond to user interactions, such as play/pause buttons or volume adjustments.

```cpp
sf::Event event;
while (window.pollEvent(event)) {
    if (event.type == sf::Event::KeyPressed) {
        if (event.key.code == sf::Keyboard::Space) {
            // Toggle play/pause
            if (sound.getStatus() == sf::Sound::Playing) {
                sound.pause();
            } else {
                sound.play();
            }
        }
    }
}
```

Video Playback with External Libraries

SFML primarily focuses on audio and graphics, so for video playback, you may need to integrate external libraries or plugins like FFmpeg or GStreamer. These libraries can decode video files and provide video frames that you can render using SFML's graphics capabilities.

Here's a simplified overview of integrating FFmpeg for video playback:

1. **Include FFmpeg Headers:** Include the necessary FFmpeg headers in your project.

```cpp
extern "C" {
#include <libavformat/avformat.h>
#include <libavcodec/avcodec.h>
```

```
#include <libswscale/swscale.h>
}
```

2. **Initialize FFmpeg:** Initialize the FFmpeg library before using it.
```
av_register_all();
avformat_network_init();
```

3. **Open Video File:** Use FFmpeg to open the video file and access its streams.
```
AVFormatContext* formatContext = avformat_alloc_context();
if (avformat_open_input(&formatContext, "video_file.mp4", NULL, NULL) != 0) {
    // Handle opening error
}
```

4. **Retrieve Video Stream Information:** Find the video stream in the format context and retrieve its codec information.
```
int videoStream = -1;
for (unsigned int i = 0; i < formatContext->nb_streams; i++) {
    if (formatContext->streams[i]->codecpar->codec_type == AVMEDIA_TYPE_VIDEO
) {
        videoStream = i;
        break;
    }
}
```

5. **Initialize Video Codec:** Initialize the video codec and create a SwsContext for frame conversion if needed.

6. **Decode and Render Frames:** Use FFmpeg to decode video frames and render them using SFML's `sf::RenderWindow`.

Please note that video playback with FFmpeg is more complex and requires handling various video formats, frame synchronization, and rendering. You may need to refer to FFmpeg documentation and tutorials for detailed implementation.

Handling audio and video playback in your multimedia player project is a crucial aspect. SFML simplifies audio playback, while for video playback, you may need to integrate external libraries like FFmpeg. By implementing these features, you can create a comprehensive multimedia player capable of playing various media formats.

Section 4.3: Implementing Playlist and Navigation Features

In this section, we will discuss how to implement playlist and navigation features in your multimedia player project using SFML. Playlists are essential for managing and playing multiple media files seamlessly. Additionally, navigation features like skip forward, skip backward, and seeking are vital for user convenience.

Designing the Playlist

Designing a playlist involves managing a list of media files that the user can select and play. Here are the key steps for implementing a playlist:

1. **Data Structure:** Choose a data structure to store the list of media files. A dynamic data structure like a linked list or vector is suitable for managing playlists.

2. **User Interface:** Create a user interface component, such as a list view or table, to display the playlist to the user. Each entry in the playlist should represent a media file.

3. **Adding and Removing Media:** Implement functionality to add media files to the playlist. Users can typically do this through a "Add to Playlist" button or drag-and-drop functionality. Likewise, provide options for removing media from the playlist.

4. **Playlist Navigation:** Allow users to navigate through the playlist, selecting the media they want to play next.

Playlist Navigation Controls

Navigation controls are essential for controlling playback within a media file and switching between files in the playlist. Here are common navigation controls you should consider implementing:

1. **Play/Pause:** A play/pause button allows users to start or pause media playback.

2. **Stop:** A stop button terminates playback and resets the media to the beginning.

3. **Next and Previous:** Buttons to skip to the next or previous media file in the playlist.

4. **Seeking:** A slider or progress bar enables users to seek to a specific point in the media file.

Code Example: Implementing Playlist and Navigation

Here's a simplified code example demonstrating how to create a playlist and implement navigation controls in a multimedia player using SFML:

```cpp
#include <SFML/Graphics.hpp>
#include <vector>
#include <iostream>

// Define a structure for playlist entries
struct PlaylistEntry {
    std::string title;
    std::string filePath;
};

int main() {
    sf::RenderWindow window(sf::VideoMode(800, 600), "Multimedia Player");
```

```cpp
    // Create a vector to store playlist entries
    std::vector<PlaylistEntry> playlist;
    playlist.push_back({ "Song 1", "song1.mp3" });
    playlist.push_back({ "Song 2", "song2.mp3" });
    playlist.push_back({ "Video 1", "video1.mp4" });

    int currentTrack = 0; // Index of the currently playing media

    while (window.isOpen()) {
        sf::Event event;
        while (window.pollEvent(event)) {
            if (event.type == sf::Event::Closed) {
                window.close();
            }

            // Handle user input for playlist navigation
            if (event.type == sf::Event::KeyPressed) {
                if (event.key.code == sf::Keyboard::Space) {
                    // Play/pause toggle
                    std::cout << "Toggling play/pause." << std::endl;
                } else if (event.key.code == sf::Keyboard::Right) {
                    // Next track
                    currentTrack = (currentTrack + 1) % playlist.size();
                    std::cout << "Playing next track: " << playlist[currentTr
ack].title << std::endl;
                } else if (event.key.code == sf::Keyboard::Left) {
                    // Previous track
                    currentTrack = (currentTrack - 1 + playlist.size()) % pla
ylist.size();
                    std::cout << "Playing previous track: " << playlist[curre
ntTrack].title << std::endl;
                }
            }
        }

        window.clear(sf::Color::Black);
        // Render playlist, navigation controls, and media playback here
        window.display();
    }

    return 0;
}
```

This code defines a playlist as a vector of PlaylistEntry structures and allows navigation through the playlist using keyboard inputs. You can expand upon this foundation to create a fully functional multimedia player with playlist management and navigation controls.

Implementing playlist and navigation features enhances the usability of your multimedia player project. Users can easily manage and control media playback, providing a more enjoyable experience when interacting with your application.

Section 4.4: Creating a Custom User Interface

In this section, we will explore the process of creating a custom user interface (UI) for your multimedia player project using SFML. While SFML provides basic graphics capabilities, creating a custom UI allows you to design a unique and user-friendly interface tailored to your application's needs.

The Importance of Custom UI

A custom UI can offer several advantages:

1. **Unique Design:** You have complete creative control over the appearance and layout of your multimedia player's interface. This enables you to design a UI that aligns with your application's branding and aesthetics.

2. **User Experience:** Custom UIs can enhance the user experience by providing intuitive and user-friendly controls. You can design UI elements that are tailored to your users' preferences and habits.

3. **Feature Integration:** A custom UI allows you to seamlessly integrate playlist management, navigation controls, and other features directly into the interface, making them easily accessible to users.

Designing Custom UI Elements

To create a custom UI, you'll need to design UI elements such as buttons, sliders, progress bars, and text labels. SFML provides the building blocks for rendering these elements, and you can implement custom logic to handle user interactions.

Custom Buttons

For custom buttons, you can create textured rectangles or sprites with SFML and detect mouse clicks within their boundaries to trigger actions. Here's a simplified example of a custom button:

```cpp
// Create a button sprite
sf::Texture buttonTexture;
if (buttonTexture.loadFromFile("button.png")) {
    sf::Sprite buttonSprite(buttonTexture);

    // Check for mouse click within the button's bounds
    if (sf::Mouse::isButtonPressed(sf::Mouse::Left) &&
        buttonSprite.getGlobalBounds().contains(sf::Mouse::getPosition(window
).x, sf::Mouse::getPosition(window).y)) {
```

```
            // Button clicked, perform action
        }

        // Render the button sprite
        window.draw(buttonSprite);
}
```

Custom Sliders and Progress Bars

To create custom sliders or progress bars, you can use rectangles or shapes as the track and a movable rectangle as the slider thumb. You'll need to handle mouse interactions for dragging the slider thumb and updating the slider's value accordingly.

Custom Text Labels

SFML's sf::Text class allows you to display custom text labels. You can set the font, size, color, and position of text labels to provide information to users or label UI elements.

Code Example: Custom Play/Pause Button

Here's an example of a custom play/pause button in SFML:

```cpp
#include <SFML/Graphics.hpp>

int main() {
    sf::RenderWindow window(sf::VideoMode(800, 600), "Custom UI Example");

    // Load play and pause button textures
    sf::Texture playTexture, pauseTexture;
    playTexture.loadFromFile("play.png");
    pauseTexture.loadFromFile("pause.png");

    sf::Sprite playButton(playTexture);
    bool isPlaying = false;

    while (window.isOpen()) {
        sf::Event event;
        while (window.pollEvent(event)) {
            if (event.type == sf::Event::Closed) {
                window.close();
            }

            // Check for mouse click within the button's bounds
            if (event.type == sf::Event::MouseButtonPressed &&
                event.mouseButton.button == sf::Mouse::Left &&
                playButton.getGlobalBounds().contains(sf::Mouse::getPosition(
window).x, sf::Mouse::getPosition(window).y)) {
                // Toggle play/pause
                isPlaying = !isPlaying;
                if (isPlaying) {
```

```
                playButton.setTexture(pauseTexture);
            } else {
                playButton.setTexture(playTexture);
            }
        }
    }

    window.clear(sf::Color::White);
    // Render other UI elements here
    window.draw(playButton);
    window.display();
    }

    return 0;
}
```

In this code, we load two textures for the play and pause buttons, detect mouse clicks within the button's bounds, and toggle between play and pause states accordingly. This demonstrates how to create a custom UI element and handle user interactions.

Creating a custom user interface for your multimedia player allows you to tailor the visual and interactive aspects of your application to meet your users' needs and expectations. By designing and implementing custom UI elements, you can enhance the user experience and create a distinctive multimedia player.

Section 4.5: Cross-Platform Deployment for the Multimedia Player

In this section, we will explore the considerations and strategies for deploying your multimedia player project across different platforms using SFML. Ensuring that your application works seamlessly on various operating systems is crucial for reaching a broad user base.

Cross-Platform Compatibility

SFML, by design, offers good cross-platform compatibility. However, there are still platform-specific differences to be aware of, such as file path conventions, window management, and input handling. To achieve true cross-platform compatibility, consider the following:

1. **Use Platform-Independent APIs:** Whenever possible, use platform-independent APIs provided by SFML. For example, use sf::VideoMode to create windows instead of platform-specific window functions.

2. **Conditional Compilation:** Use conditional compilation directives (#ifdef, #elif, #else) to include platform-specific code sections when necessary. This allows you to write platform-specific code within a single codebase.

3. **Test on Multiple Platforms:** Regularly test your multimedia player on various platforms, including Windows, macOS, and Linux. This helps identify and resolve platform-specific issues early in the development process.

4. **File Path Handling:** Be mindful of file path conventions. Use SFML's `sf::String` and `sf::String::fromUtf8` functions to convert file paths as needed to ensure compatibility across platforms.

Building for Different Platforms

To build and package your multimedia player for different platforms, you'll need to consider the following:

1. **Compilers and Build Tools:** Use the appropriate compilers and build tools for each platform. For example, Visual Studio for Windows, Xcode for macOS, and GNU Make for Linux.

2. **Static vs. Dynamic Linking:** Decide whether to statically or dynamically link SFML libraries. Statically linking includes SFML libraries within your executable, while dynamic linking relies on external library files. Your choice may depend on distribution and deployment preferences.

3. **Platform-Specific Dependencies:** Be aware of any platform-specific dependencies your multimedia player may have. For instance, if you're using external libraries like FFmpeg, ensure that the necessary libraries and plugins are available on each platform.

4. **Packaging and Distribution:** Prepare installation packages or distributions tailored to each platform's packaging conventions. For Windows, this may involve creating an installer package. For macOS, consider creating a DMG file. For Linux, provide packages for popular package managers or distribution-specific formats.

Code Example: Cross-Platform File Path Handling

Handling file paths in a cross-platform manner is crucial. Here's a code example that demonstrates how to convert file paths to UTF-8 for Windows and use the original path for other platforms:

```cpp
#include <SFML/System.hpp>
#include <iostream>

int main() {
    std::string path = "C:\\Users\\User\\Documents\\file.txt";

#ifdef _WIN32
    // Convert path to UTF-8 for Windows
    sf::String utf8Path = sf::String::fromUtf8(path.begin(), path.end());
    std::cout << "UTF-8 Path: " << utf8Path.toUtf8() << std::endl;
#else
```

```
    // Use the original path for other platforms
    std::cout << "Path: " << path << std::endl;
#endif

    return 0;
}
```

In this code, the file path is converted to UTF-8 for Windows using SFML's sf::String::fromUtf8 function, ensuring that it's compatible with SFML's file operations.

Ensuring cross-platform deployment is a crucial step in making your multimedia player accessible to a wide audience. By following best practices, testing on multiple platforms, and handling platform-specific considerations, you can successfully deploy your multimedia player on various operating systems.

Chapter 5: Advanced Input Handling and Interaction

Section 5.1: Designing Complex User Interfaces

In this section, we will explore the principles and techniques for designing complex user interfaces (UIs) in your multimedia player project using SFML. Complex UIs often involve multiple elements, user interactions, and a cohesive design that enhances user experience.

Importance of Complex UIs

Complex UIs are essential for multimedia players because they provide users with the tools and features they need to control and interact with various media types effectively. Here are some reasons why complex UIs matter:

1. **User Control:** Complex UIs enable users to have fine-grained control over playback, navigation, and customization of their multimedia experience.

2. **Feature Accessibility:** They make it easier to access advanced features like playlist management, audio settings, visualizations, and more.

3. **Intuitive Interaction:** A well-designed complex UI ensures that users can intuitively understand and use the interface, even with multiple features and options available.

Designing Complex UI Elements

To design complex UI elements, consider the following principles:

1. **Hierarchy and Organization:** Group related UI elements together and establish a clear hierarchy. For example, place playback controls near the media player, and keep settings and preferences separate.

2. **Consistency:** Maintain consistency in design elements, such as button styles, fonts, and color schemes, to create a cohesive look and feel.

3. **User Feedback:** Provide visual and auditory feedback to inform users about the system's state. For instance, highlight the currently playing media or display progress visually.

4. **Responsive Design:** Ensure that your UI elements adapt to different screen sizes and resolutions, accommodating a wide range of devices and platforms.

5. **User Testing:** Conduct usability testing to gather feedback from actual users. This helps identify pain points and areas for improvement in your complex UI.

Code Example: Creating a Complex Playlist UI

Let's consider a code example for creating a complex playlist UI in SFML. This UI may include features like adding/removing items, reordering entries, and displaying additional information about each media file:

```cpp
#include <SFML/Graphics.hpp>
#include <vector>
#include <iostream>

struct PlaylistEntry {
    std::string title;
    std::string filePath;
};

int main() {
    sf::RenderWindow window(sf::VideoMode(800, 600), "Complex Playlist UI Exa
mple");

    std::vector<PlaylistEntry> playlist; // Vector to store playlist entries

    while (window.isOpen()) {
        sf::Event event;
        while (window.pollEvent(event)) {
            if (event.type == sf::Event::Closed) {
                window.close();
            }

            // Handle user interactions for the playlist UI
            if (event.type == sf::Event::MouseButtonPressed &&
                event.mouseButton.button == sf::Mouse::Left) {
                // Check if a playlist item was clicked and perform actions
                for (size_t i = 0; i < playlist.size(); i++) {
                    // Check if the mouse click is within the bounds of the p
laylist item
                    if (/* Mouse position within playlist item bounds */) {
                        // Handle playlist item click
                        std::cout << "Clicked on playlist item: " << playlist
[i].title << std::endl;
                        break;
                    }
                }
            }
        }

        window.clear(sf::Color::White);
        // Render the playlist UI elements here
        window.display();
    }
}
```

```
    return 0;
}
```

In this code example, we create a playlist UI that allows users to interact with playlist entries by clicking on them. You can expand upon this foundation to create a more advanced and visually appealing complex UI for your multimedia player.

Designing complex UIs for your multimedia player enhances user experience and provides users with the tools and features they need to interact with multimedia content effectively. By following design principles and considering user feedback, you can create an engaging and user-friendly interface.

Section 5.2: Handling Multitouch Input

In this section, we will explore the topic of handling multitouch input in your multimedia player project using SFML. Multitouch support is essential for modern user interfaces, especially on touch-enabled devices such as tablets and smartphones. It allows users to interact with the application using multiple touch points simultaneously.

The Significance of Multitouch

Multitouch input enables a more intuitive and interactive user experience. Some key advantages of multitouch support include:

1. **Gesture Recognition:** Multitouch allows you to recognize complex gestures like pinch-to-zoom, swipe, and rotate. These gestures enhance the usability and functionality of your multimedia player.

2. **Efficient Interaction:** Users can perform multiple actions at once, making it easier to control playback, adjust settings, and navigate through content.

3. **Natural Interaction:** Multitouch mimics real-world interactions, making the application feel more intuitive and engaging.

Handling Multitouch in SFML

SFML provides support for handling multitouch input through its `sf::Touch` class. Here's an overview of how to handle multitouch input:

1. **Enable Multitouch:** To enable multitouch support, call `sf::Touch::setSensitivity(float)` with a sensitivity value greater than 1.0. This value determines the number of pixels the touch point must move before SFML considers it a new touch event.

2. **Poll for Touch Events:** In your main loop, you can poll for touch events using `sf::Touch::isDown(int)` to check if a touch point is down. You can also retrieve the position of a touch point using `sf::Touch::getPosition(int)`.

3. **Recognize Gestures:** Implement gesture recognition by tracking the movement and state of multiple touch points. For example, you can detect pinch gestures by measuring the distance between two touch points over time.

Code Example: Pinch-to-Zoom Gesture

Here's a simplified code example that demonstrates how to implement a pinch-to-zoom gesture in SFML:

```cpp
#include <SFML/Graphics.hpp>
#include <iostream>

int main() {
    sf::RenderWindow window(sf::VideoMode(800, 600), "Multitouch Example");
    sf::CircleShape circle(50);
    circle.setFillColor(sf::Color::Blue);

    sf::Touch::setSensitivity(1.0f); // Enable multitouch

    while (window.isOpen()) {
        sf::Event event;
        while (window.pollEvent(event)) {
            if (event.type == sf::Event::Closed) {
                window.close();
            }

            // Handle multitouch events
            if (event.type == sf::Event::TouchBegan) {
                // Touch point down
                std::cout << "Touch Began at (" << event.touch.x << ", " << event.touch.y << ")" << std::endl;
            } else if (event.type == sf::Event::TouchMoved) {
                // Touch point moved
                std::cout << "Touch Moved to (" << event.touch.x << ", " << event.touch.y << ")" << std::endl;
            } else if (event.type == sf::Event::TouchEnded) {
                // Touch point released
                std::cout << "Touch Ended" << std::endl;
            }
        }

        window.clear();
        // Update and draw UI elements here
        window.draw(circle);
        window.display();
    }

    return 0;
}
```

In this code, we enable multitouch support, and when users perform touch events, we detect and print their positions. You can adapt this foundation to recognize more complex gestures, such as pinch-to-zoom, by tracking the movement of multiple touch points.

Implementing multitouch support in your multimedia player project enhances user interaction and makes your application more versatile, especially on touch-enabled devices. By recognizing gestures and providing natural touch interactions, you can create a more engaging user experience.

Section 5.3: Gesture Recognition and Processing

In this section, we delve into the topic of gesture recognition and processing for your multimedia player project using SFML. Gesture recognition allows your application to interpret complex user actions, making the user experience more interactive and intuitive.

The Role of Gesture Recognition

Gesture recognition plays a crucial role in enhancing user interaction and control in multimedia applications. Here are some key points to consider:

1. **Improved User Experience:** Gesture recognition enables users to interact with your multimedia player in a natural and intuitive way. Recognizing gestures like swipes, pinches, and rotations makes the user experience smoother and more enjoyable.

2. **Complex Interactions:** Gesture recognition allows your application to interpret complex user actions. For example, recognizing a swipe gesture can trigger actions such as changing tracks, adjusting volume, or navigating through playlists.

3. **Touchscreen Devices:** On touchscreen devices like smartphones and tablets, gesture recognition is essential for providing touch-based navigation and control.

Implementing Gesture Recognition in SFML

SFML provides the tools and events necessary to implement gesture recognition in your multimedia player. Here's a high-level overview of how to approach gesture recognition:

1. **Enable Touch Events:** Enable multitouch support using `sf::Touch::setSensitivity(float)`, as discussed in the previous section.

2. **Detect Gesture Events:** SFML generates gesture events when it recognizes specific gestures. You can handle these events to trigger actions in response to gestures.

3. **Gesture Event Types:** SFML defines several gesture event types, including `sf::Event::GestureBegan`, `sf::Event::GestureMoved`, and `sf::Event::GestureEnded`. These events provide information about the gesture, such as its type, position, and scale.

4. **Gesture Attributes:** Each gesture event contains attributes specific to the recognized gesture. For example, a pinch gesture event provides information about the scale factor, which you can use to implement pinch-to-zoom functionality.

Code Example: Pinch-to-Zoom Gesture

Let's expand on the pinch-to-zoom gesture example from the previous section and add gesture recognition to it:

```cpp
#include <SFML/Graphics.hpp>
#include <iostream>

int main() {
    sf::RenderWindow window(sf::VideoMode(800, 600), "Gesture Recognition Exa
mple");
    sf::CircleShape circle(50);
    circle.setFillColor(sf::Color::Blue);

    sf::Touch::setSensitivity(1.0f); // Enable multitouch

    while (window.isOpen()) {
        sf::Event event;
        while (window.pollEvent(event)) {
            if (event.type == sf::Event::Closed) {
                window.close();
            }

            // Handle multitouch events
            if (event.type == sf::Event::TouchBegan) {
                // Touch point down
                std::cout << "Touch Began at (" << event.touch.x << ", " << e
vent.touch.y << ")" << std::endl;
            } else if (event.type == sf::Event::GestureBegan) {
                // Gesture recognition started
                std::cout << "Gesture Began: Type " << event.gesture.type <<
std::endl;
            } else if (event.type == sf::Event::GestureUpdated) {
                // Gesture in progress
                std::cout << "Gesture Updated: Type " << event.gesture.type <
< std::endl;
            } else if (event.type == sf::Event::GestureEnded) {
                // Gesture recognition completed
                std::cout << "Gesture Ended: Type " << event.gesture.type <<
std::endl;
            }
        }

        window.clear();
        // Update and draw UI elements here
        window.draw(circle);
```

```
      window.display();
   }

   return 0;
}
```

In this code, we handle gesture events alongside touch events. When a gesture begins, is updated, or ends, we print information about the gesture, such as its type. This demonstrates how to incorporate gesture recognition into your multimedia player project.

Gesture recognition enriches the user experience in your multimedia player by allowing users to perform complex actions with natural gestures. By implementing gesture recognition using SFML, you can create an interactive and user-friendly application that responds to the way users interact with touch-enabled devices.

Section 5.4: Implementing Advanced Mouse and Keyboard Interactions

In this section, we will explore advanced techniques for handling mouse and keyboard interactions in your multimedia player project using SFML. These interactions are essential for providing users with precise control and customization options.

Importance of Advanced Input Handling

Advanced mouse and keyboard interactions play a crucial role in multimedia players, especially when users want to control various aspects of media playback, navigation, and customization. Here's why advanced input handling is important:

1. **Precision Control:** Advanced input techniques allow users to precisely control playback, volume, and other settings, enhancing the overall experience.

2. **Customization:** Users can interact with UI elements, adjust audio settings, and navigate playlists more efficiently, making it easier to tailor their multimedia experience.

3. **User-Friendly Interface:** Well-designed mouse and keyboard interactions contribute to a user-friendly interface, ensuring that users can intuitively interact with your multimedia player.

Implementing Advanced Mouse Interactions

To implement advanced mouse interactions in your multimedia player, consider the following techniques:

1. **Custom Mouse Cursors:** Change the mouse cursor to provide visual feedback when hovering over interactive UI elements, such as buttons or sliders.

2. **Drag-and-Drop:** Implement drag-and-drop functionality for playlist management or reordering items.

3. **Context Menus:** Create context menus that appear when right-clicking on items, allowing users to access additional options.

4. **Mouse Wheel:** Utilize the mouse wheel for functions like volume control or timeline scrubbing.

Implementing Advanced Keyboard Interactions

Advanced keyboard interactions can greatly improve the user experience. Here are some techniques to consider:

1. **Keyboard Shortcuts:** Implement keyboard shortcuts for common actions, such as play/pause, next/previous track, and volume control.

2. **Search and Navigation:** Allow users to search for media files or navigate through playlists using keyboard input.

3. **Hotkeys:** Enable users to customize hotkeys for specific functions, providing a personalized experience.

Code Example: Custom Mouse Cursor

Here's a simple code example that demonstrates how to change the mouse cursor when hovering over a button in SFML:

```cpp
#include <SFML/Graphics.hpp>

int main() {
    sf::RenderWindow window(sf::VideoMode(800, 600), "Custom Mouse Cursor Example");

    // Load a custom mouse cursor image
    sf::Texture cursorTexture;
    cursorTexture.loadFromFile("cursor.png");
    sf::Cursor customCursor;
    customCursor.loadFromPixels(cursorTexture.copyToImage().getPixelsPtr(), {32, 32}, {0, 0});

    // Create a button
    sf::RectangleShape button(sf::Vector2f(200, 50));
    button.setPosition(300, 300);
    button.setFillColor(sf::Color::Blue);

    while (window.isOpen()) {
        sf::Event event;
        while (window.pollEvent(event)) {
            if (event.type == sf::Event::Closed) {
                window.close();
            }
```

```
            // Change the mouse cursor when hovering over the button
            if (event.type == sf::Event::MouseMoved) {
                if (button.getGlobalBounds().contains(sf::Vector2f(event.mous
eMove.x, event.mouseMove.y))) {
                    window.setMouseCursor(customCursor);
                } else {
                    window.setMouseCursor(sf::Cursor::Arrow);
                }
            }
        }

        window.clear();
        // Draw UI elements here
        window.draw(button);
        window.display();
    }

    return 0;
}
```

In this code, we load a custom mouse cursor image and change the mouse cursor to the custom cursor when the mouse hovers over a button. This demonstrates how you can provide visual feedback to users during mouse interactions.

Implementing advanced mouse and keyboard interactions in your multimedia player project enhances user control and customization, resulting in a more user-friendly and versatile application. By incorporating these techniques, you can create an engaging and efficient multimedia player that caters to a wide range of user preferences.

Section 5.5: Creating Custom Input Devices Integration

In this section, we will explore the concept of creating custom input devices integration for your multimedia player project using SFML. Custom input devices can enhance user interactions and provide unique ways to control and navigate your application.

The Potential of Custom Input Devices

Integrating custom input devices offers several advantages for your multimedia player:

1. **Innovative Interactions:** Custom input devices can introduce innovative and unconventional ways for users to interact with your application. This can set your multimedia player apart from others in terms of user experience.

2. **Accessibility:** Some users may have specific input needs due to physical limitations. Custom input devices can make your application more accessible to a broader audience.

3. **Specialized Functionality:** Depending on the nature of your multimedia player, custom input devices can offer specialized functionality. For example, you can create a custom controller for music production or DJing.

Integrating custom input devices into your multimedia player typically involves the following steps:

1. **Device Compatibility:** Identify the custom input device you want to integrate and ensure that it is compatible with your platform and system.

2. **Device Communication:** Establish communication between your application and the custom input device. This may involve using device-specific libraries or protocols.

3. **Event Handling:** Implement event handlers or listeners to capture input from the custom device. Map the device's inputs (e.g., buttons, sensors) to specific actions in your multimedia player.

4. **User Configuration:** Provide users with the option to configure and customize the behavior of the custom input device within your application.

Code Example: Integrating a MIDI Controller

Here's a simplified code example that demonstrates how to integrate a MIDI controller into your multimedia player using the SFML library. In this example, we'll assume the MIDI controller sends MIDI note-on and note-off messages, which we'll use to control media playback:

```cpp
#include <SFML/Graphics.hpp>
#include <iostream>

// Function to handle MIDI note-on messages
void handleMIDINoteOn(int note) {
    std::cout << "MIDI Note On: " << note << std::endl;
    // Implement playback control or other actions here
}

// Function to handle MIDI note-off messages
void handleMIDINoteOff(int note) {
    std::cout << "MIDI Note Off: " << note << std::endl;
    // Implement playback control or other actions here
}

int main() {
    // Initialize SFML window and multimedia player

    while (window.isOpen()) {
        sf::Event event;
```

```
    while (window.pollEvent(event)) {
        if (event.type == sf::Event::Closed) {
            window.close();
        }

        // Handle MIDI messages from the custom input device
        if (event.type == sf::Event::Custom) {
            if (event.custom.code == MIDI_NOTE_ON) {
                int note = event.custom.data1;
                handleMIDINoteOn(note);
            } else if (event.custom.code == MIDI_NOTE_OFF) {
                int note = event.custom.data1;
                handleMIDINoteOff(note);
            }
        }
    }

    // Update and draw UI elements here
    window.display();
}

    return 0;
}
```

In this code example, we handle MIDI note-on and note-off messages from a custom MIDI controller. These messages are used to trigger actions within the multimedia player, such as playback control. You can adapt this code to integrate other custom input devices based on your project's requirements.

Integrating custom input devices into your multimedia player project allows you to offer unique and tailored user experiences. Whether it's for specialized functionality, accessibility, or innovation, custom input device integration can set your application apart and provide users with new and exciting ways to interact with multimedia content.

Chapter 6: Developing a Cross-Platform Game Engine

Section 6.1: Building the Foundation of a Game Engine

In this section, we will delve into the process of building the foundation of a cross-platform game engine using SFML. A game engine serves as the core framework for game development, providing the necessary structure and tools for creating games efficiently and effectively.

The Role of a Game Engine Foundation

The foundation of a game engine is crucial, as it lays the groundwork for the entire game development process. Here are some key aspects to consider when building this foundation:

1. **Abstraction of Low-Level Details:** A game engine abstracts low-level details, such as hardware-specific operations and input handling, allowing game developers to focus on game logic and content.

2. **Graphics and Rendering:** The engine foundation typically includes a graphics subsystem for rendering 2D or 3D graphics. It manages rendering resources, handles animations, and optimizes performance.

3. **Audio Management:** Sound and music are essential components of games. The foundation should include an audio system to manage audio assets, playback, and effects.

4. **Input Handling:** Managing user input from various devices (keyboard, mouse, gamepad) is a critical part of the foundation. It provides a consistent interface for handling input across platforms.

5. **Event Systems:** Game events and interactions are managed through event systems. These systems handle player actions, collisions, and other game events.

Building the Foundation with SFML

SFML is a versatile library for building the foundation of your game engine. It provides the following features:

- **Graphics:** SFML offers 2D graphics rendering capabilities with support for textures, sprites, and more. You can create visually appealing games with ease.

- **Audio:** SFML includes a simple and efficient audio system for managing sound effects and music playback.

- **Input Handling:** SFML simplifies input handling by providing intuitive interfaces for keyboard, mouse, joystick, and touchscreen inputs.

- **Window Management:** The library manages windows and their events, making it easy to create cross-platform game windows.

Here's a simplified example of setting up a game engine foundation using SFML:

```cpp
#include <SFML/Graphics.hpp>
#include <SFML/Audio.hpp>

int main() {
    // Create a game window
    sf::RenderWindow window(sf::VideoMode(800, 600), "My Game");

    // Initialize game resources (textures, fonts, audio, etc.)

    // Main game loop
    while (window.isOpen()) {
        sf::Event event;
        while (window.pollEvent(event)) {
            if (event.type == sf::Event::Closed) {
                window.close();
            }

            // Handle other game events here
        }

        // Update game logic, physics, and animations

        // Clear the window
        window.clear();

        // Draw game objects and graphics

        // Display the frame
        window.display();
    }

    // Clean up and exit
    return 0;
}
```

In this code example, we create a game window, handle events, update game logic, and render graphics using SFML. This is the fundamental structure you'll build upon when developing your cross-platform game engine. The engine's foundation sets the stage for creating exciting and interactive games across various platforms.

Section 6.2: Abstracting Graphics and Audio Systems

In this section, we will explore the abstraction of graphics and audio systems in the development of a cross-platform game engine using SFML. Abstraction is a crucial concept in game engine design as it allows developers to work with high-level interfaces while hiding platform-specific details.

Abstracting the Graphics System

When building a game engine, it's essential to abstract the graphics system to provide a unified interface for rendering graphics, regardless of the underlying platform. This abstraction simplifies the development process and ensures cross-platform compatibility.

In your game engine, you can create a GraphicsManager or Renderer class responsible for handling all rendering tasks. This class should provide functions to load and manage textures, sprites, shaders, and other graphics resources. Here's a simplified example:

```cpp
class GraphicsManager {
public:
    // Load a texture from a file
    bool loadTexture(const std::string& filename, const std::string& id);

    // Draw a sprite to the screen
    void drawSprite(const std::string& textureId, const sf::Vector2f& position);

    // Apply a shader
    void applyShader(const sf::Shader& shader);

    // Other graphics-related functions...

private:
    std::map<std::string, sf::Texture> textures;
    std::vector<sf::Sprite> sprites;
};
```

By creating this abstraction, game developers using your engine can load textures, draw sprites, and apply shaders without worrying about the platform-specific implementation details. Under the hood, you'll implement these functions using SFML's graphics capabilities.

Abstracting the Audio System

Similar to graphics, abstracting the audio system is essential for a cross-platform game engine. Your AudioManager class should handle audio assets, playback, and effects. Here's a simplified example:

```cpp
class AudioManager {
public:
    // Load a sound from a file
    bool loadSound(const std::string& filename, const std::string& id);

    // Play a sound
    void playSound(const std::string& soundId);

    // Adjust volume and other audio properties

    // Other audio-related functions...

private:
    std::map<std::string, sf::SoundBuffer> soundBuffers;
    std::map<std::string, sf::Sound> sounds;
};
```

With this abstraction, game developers can easily load and play sounds in their games without worrying about the platform-specific audio APIs. SFML's audio capabilities will be utilized behind the scenes.

Platform-Specific Implementations

Underneath these abstraction layers, you'll implement platform-specific code to make everything work seamlessly on different platforms. For example, on Windows, you'll use Direct3D for graphics rendering, while on macOS, you'll utilize OpenGL. SFML handles these platform-specific details, allowing you to focus on the higher-level abstractions.

In summary, abstracting the graphics and audio systems in your game engine is crucial for providing a clean and unified interface to game developers. It simplifies game development and ensures cross-platform compatibility, allowing games to run smoothly on various operating systems.

Section 6.3: Implementing Input Handling and Event Systems

In this section, we will explore the implementation of input handling and event systems in the development of a cross-platform game engine using SFML. Managing user input and handling events is a critical aspect of game development, and having a well-structured system ensures a smooth player experience.

Input Handling

Game engines need to provide a unified way to handle input from various devices like keyboards, mice, gamepads, and touchscreens. SFML simplifies this process by offering a unified interface for input.

Here's a basic outline of how you can implement input handling in your game engine:

1. **Initialization:** Set up the input system during the engine's initialization phase. Create input manager classes that abstract input devices. Initialize input devices such as keyboards, mice, and gamepads.

2. **Polling Input:** In the game loop, poll input events using SFML's event system. For example, you can use `sf::Event` to check for keyboard or mouse events:

```
sf::Event event;
while (window.pollEvent(event)) {
    if (event.type == sf::Event::KeyPressed) {
        // Handle key press
    }
    else if (event.type == sf::Event::MouseButtonPressed) {
        // Handle mouse button press
    }
    // Handle other events...
}
```

3. **Abstracted Input:** Use abstracted input functions to provide a simplified interface for game developers. For instance, create functions like `IsKeyPressed`, `IsMouseButtonPressed`, or `GetMousePosition` that internally utilize SFML's input events.

4. **Input States:** Maintain input states to handle continuous input. Track which keys are held down or which buttons are continuously pressed to handle actions like character movement or continuous firing in a game.

Event Systems

Events are essential for handling interactions in games, such as collisions, user interactions, or game state changes. Designing a flexible event system is crucial for a game engine.

Here's how you can implement an event system:

1. **Event Manager:** Create an event manager class responsible for managing and dispatching events. Game objects can register themselves as event listeners with the event manager.

2. **Event Types:** Define a set of event types that cover different game scenarios, such as collisions, user input, or level changes.

3. **Event Listeners:** Game objects, like characters or items, can register as event listeners with the event manager. They specify which types of events they want to listen to.

4. **Dispatch Events:** When a relevant game event occurs, dispatch it to all registered event listeners. For example, when two game objects collide, an event is created and dispatched to notify the objects involved.

Here's a simplified example of an event manager implementation:

```
class EventManager {
public:
    // Register an object as an event listener for a specific event type
    void AddListener(GameObject* listener, EventType eventType);

    // Remove an object from the list of event listeners
    void RemoveListener(GameObject* listener, EventType eventType);

    // Dispatch an event to all registered listeners of a specific type
    void DispatchEvent(EventType eventType, EventData eventData);

private:
    std::map<EventType, std::vector<GameObject*>> listeners;
};
```

By implementing input handling and event systems in your game engine, you provide a structured way for game developers to create interactive and responsive games. These systems abstract the complexities of handling user input and game events, allowing developers to focus on game logic and mechanics.

Section 6.4: Developing Cross-Platform Game Logic

In this section, we will explore the development of cross-platform game logic within the context of building a game engine using SFML. Game logic forms the heart of any game, defining how the game behaves and responds to player actions. Ensuring that this game logic is cross-platform compatible is crucial for creating games that run smoothly on various operating systems.

Abstraction of Game Logic

Game logic encompasses a wide range of functionalities, including character movement, physics simulations, enemy behavior, game rules, and win/lose conditions. When developing a game engine, it's essential to abstract the game logic in a way that isolates it from platform-specific concerns.

To achieve this abstraction:

1. **Encapsulation:** Encapsulate game logic within classes or modules that are platform-independent. For example, create classes like Player, Enemy, and GameWorld that handle their respective logic.

2. **Input-Output Separation:** Separate the game's input and output from its core logic. Input should be abstracted through the input handling system discussed earlier. Output, such as rendering and audio, should also be abstracted through appropriate subsystems.

3. **Cross-Platform Libraries:** Utilize cross-platform libraries and APIs for tasks like random number generation, file I/O, and date/time handling. This ensures that these critical aspects of game logic work consistently across different platforms.

Game Loop

The game loop is a fundamental component of game logic. It defines the sequence of actions that occur in each frame of the game. A typical game loop consists of the following steps:

1. **Input Handling:** Collect and process user input, such as keyboard and mouse actions. Utilize the input handling system you've implemented earlier.

2. **Update Game State:** Update the state of game objects, including player characters, enemies, and other entities. This step involves applying physics, AI, and game rules.

3. **Collision Detection:** Detect and resolve collisions between game objects. Ensure that collision handling is consistent across platforms.

4. **Rendering:** Render the updated game state to the screen using the graphics subsystem. This step should abstract the rendering process for cross-platform compatibility.

5. **Audio:** Play audio effects and music as needed. Utilize the audio subsystem to manage sound and music assets.

6. **Timing:** Maintain a consistent frame rate and timing. Cross-platform game engines often use timing mechanisms that work uniformly across different platforms.

Here's a simplified example of a game loop structure using SFML:

```
while (window.isOpen()) {
    sf::Event event;
    while (window.pollEvent(event)) {
        if (event.type == sf::Event::Closed) {
            window.close();
        }
        // Handle other input events...
    }

    // Update game state
    UpdateGame();

    // Render game objects
    RenderGame();

    // Play audio
    PlayAudio();

    // Maintain frame rate
```

```
    MaintainFrameRate();
}
```

By abstracting game logic and following a well-structured game loop, you can ensure that your game engine's core functionality remains consistent across different platforms. This abstraction allows game developers to focus on creating engaging gameplay experiences without being hindered by platform-specific challenges.

Section 6.5: Extending the Game Engine with Advanced Features

In this section, we will delve into the process of extending your cross-platform game engine with advanced features. Building a game engine is an ongoing endeavor, and adding advanced capabilities can set your engine apart and make it more appealing to game developers.

Plugin Architecture

To make your game engine extensible and capable of accommodating new features, consider implementing a plugin architecture. This allows developers to create and integrate custom functionality seamlessly. Here's a basic outline of how you can implement a plugin system:

1. **Plugin Interface:** Define a plugin interface that outlines the methods and data structures plugins must implement or adhere to. For example, you might have a `GamePlugin` interface that includes functions like `Initialize`, `Update`, and `Render`.

2. **Dynamic Loading:** Implement dynamic loading of plugins at runtime. This enables developers to create plugins without modifying the core engine code. On platforms like Windows, you can use dynamic link libraries (DLLs) for this purpose.

3. **Plugin Manager:** Create a plugin manager responsible for discovering, loading, and managing plugins. The manager should handle initialization, updates, and shutdown procedures for each plugin.

4. **Communication:** Establish a communication mechanism between the core engine and plugins. This allows plugins to interact with the engine and vice versa. Consider using event-based communication or well-defined interfaces.

Example: Extending with Scripting

One powerful way to extend your game engine is by adding scripting support. Scripting allows game developers to define game logic, behavior, and even create custom game objects using a scripting language like Lua or Python.

Here's a simplified example of how you can integrate scripting into your game engine:

1. **Scripting Language Integration:** Choose a scripting language and integrate it into your engine. For example, you might use the Lua scripting language, which is known for its simplicity and performance.

2. **Script Execution:** Allow scripts to be loaded and executed within the engine. Create a scripting manager responsible for managing script execution.

3. **Scriptable Game Objects:** Define a mechanism for creating scriptable game objects. Game developers can attach scripts to game objects and define their behavior using scripts.

4. **Exposed API:** Expose a subset of your engine's API to the scripting environment. This enables scripts to interact with the engine's core functionality, such as accessing game object properties, triggering events, or modifying game state.

Here's a simplified example of a Lua script attached to a game object:

```lua
-- Define a script for a game object
function Initialize()
    -- Initialization code
end

function Update()
    -- Per-frame update code
    -- Move the object, react to events, etc.
end

function OnDestroy()
    -- Cleanup code when the object is destroyed
end
```

By adding scripting support, you empower game developers to customize and extend your engine's functionality without requiring changes to the engine's source code.

Advanced Physics and Rendering Techniques

Consider incorporating advanced physics and rendering techniques into your engine. This may involve adding support for physics simulations like rigid body dynamics, soft body simulations, or particle systems. You can also explore advanced rendering techniques such as deferred rendering, shadow mapping, or physically-based rendering (PBR).

To implement these features, you'll need to dive deeper into the underlying graphics and physics APIs, ensuring that these advanced capabilities remain cross-platform compatible.

By extending your game engine with advanced features, you make it a versatile tool for game developers. These features can be the key differentiators that attract developers looking to create unique and engaging games. Keep in mind that continuous improvement and community feedback are essential for the long-term success of your game engine.

Chapter 7: Abstracting SFML for Modular Development

Section 7.1: The Importance of Abstraction in Software Development

Abstraction is a fundamental concept in software development, and it plays a pivotal role in creating modular and maintainable code. In this section, we'll explore the significance of abstraction within the context of developing applications and games using the SFML library.

What Is Abstraction?

At its core, abstraction involves simplifying complex systems by focusing on the essential aspects while hiding the unnecessary details. It allows developers to work with high-level, understandable representations of concepts and functionality.

In software development, abstraction can take many forms:

1. **Data Abstraction:** Encapsulating data structures and variables, exposing only necessary information, and providing operations to manipulate them. For instance, creating a class to represent a game character's attributes and behavior.

2. **Functional Abstraction:** Defining functions or methods that perform specific tasks without exposing their inner workings. Developers can use these functions without needing to understand their implementation details.

3. **Interface Abstraction:** Creating well-defined interfaces or APIs that allow different parts of a program to interact without knowing the specifics of each other's implementations. This promotes code reusability and modular development.

Benefits of Abstraction

The benefits of abstraction in software development are numerous:

1. **Simplicity:** Abstraction simplifies complex systems, making them easier to understand and manage. This is particularly crucial when working with large codebases or collaborative projects.

2. **Modularity:** Abstraction promotes modularity by breaking down a system into smaller, manageable components. Each component can be developed, tested, and maintained independently.

3. **Reusability:** Abstraction encourages the creation of reusable components and libraries. When you abstract functionality into reusable modules, you can leverage them across various projects.

4. **Maintenance:** Abstraction reduces the complexity of code, making it easier to maintain and update. When changes are required, you can focus on the relevant abstracted components without affecting the entire system.

When working with SFML, abstraction can be applied in various ways:

1. **Graphics Abstraction:** Encapsulate SFML's graphics functions into higher-level classes or modules. For instance, create a `SpriteRenderer` class that abstracts the rendering of game sprites. This allows game developers to work with game objects and sprites without delving into the low-level details of rendering.

2. **Input Abstraction:** Abstract input handling by creating a custom input manager that provides a simplified interface for handling user input events. This shields game logic from platform-specific input details.

3. **Resource Management:** Abstract resource loading and management. Develop a resource manager that handles loading textures, sounds, and other assets. Game developers can then access these resources through a clean interface.

Here's an example of how abstraction can be applied to simplify input handling using SFML:

```cpp
class InputManager {
public:
    // Abstracted input methods
    bool IsKeyPressed(sf::Keyboard::Key key) {
        return sf::Keyboard::isKeyPressed(key);
    }

    sf::Vector2f GetMousePosition() {
        return sf::Vector2f(sf::Mouse::getPosition(window));
    }

private:
    sf::RenderWindow& window; // Reference to the SFML window
};
```

In this example, the `InputManager` abstracts input handling, providing a clear and simple interface for accessing keyboard and mouse input without exposing the SFML-specific details. Such abstractions enhance code clarity, maintainability, and portability across different platforms.

Conclusion

Abstraction is a powerful tool in software development, allowing developers to create modular, maintainable, and reusable code. When working with SFML, applying abstraction to graphics, input handling, and resource management can simplify the development process and enhance cross-platform compatibility. By abstracting SFML, you provide a clean and user-friendly interface for game developers, making it easier for them to focus on creating engaging games without being bogged down by low-level details.

Section 7.2: Designing Modular Components in SFML

When developing applications and games with the Simple and Fast Multimedia Library (SFML), designing modular components is essential for creating maintainable and extensible codebases. In this section, we'll explore the principles and techniques for designing modular components in SFML-based projects.

The Importance of Modularity

Modularity is a software design approach that involves breaking down a complex system into smaller, self-contained, and reusable components or modules. In the context of SFML development, modularity offers several benefits:

1. **Code Reusability:** Modular components can be reused across different parts of your project or in entirely new projects. This reduces code duplication and saves development time.

2. **Ease of Maintenance:** Smaller, focused modules are easier to maintain and debug than monolithic codebases. When an issue arises, you can isolate it to a specific module, making troubleshooting more efficient.

3. **Collaboration:** Modular code facilitates collaboration among team members. Developers can work on different modules independently, minimizing conflicts and merge issues.

4. **Scalability:** As your project grows, modular components can be added or modified without affecting the entire codebase. This scalability is crucial for both small and large projects.

Designing Modular Components

To design modular components effectively in SFML-based projects, consider the following principles:

1. **Single Responsibility Principle (SRP):** Each module should have a single responsibility or purpose. For example, you might have separate modules for rendering, input handling, audio playback, and game logic.

2. **Encapsulation:** Encapsulate the internal state and functionality of each module. Expose only the necessary interfaces or APIs to interact with the module. This prevents unintended access and modification of internal data.

3. **Dependency Management:** Clearly define dependencies between modules. Ensure that modules are loosely coupled, meaning they rely on well-defined interfaces rather than concrete implementations. This allows you to swap out modules or extend functionality without breaking other parts of the code.

4. **Configuration and Customization:** Provide mechanisms for configuring and customizing module behavior. This might involve using configuration files, callback functions, or dependency injection to tailor module functionality to specific requirements.

Example: Modular Graphics Rendering

Let's consider an example of designing a modular graphics rendering component in SFML:

```cpp
// GraphicsRenderer.hpp

class GraphicsRenderer {
public:
    // Constructor takes an SFML RenderWindow
    GraphicsRenderer(sf::RenderWindow& window);

    // Method to render game objects
    void RenderGameObject(const GameObject& gameObject);

private:
    sf::RenderWindow& window;
};

// GraphicsRenderer.cpp

GraphicsRenderer::GraphicsRenderer(sf::RenderWindow& window) : window(window)
{}

void GraphicsRenderer::RenderGameObject(const GameObject& gameObject) {
    // Render the game object using SFML graphics functions
    window.draw(gameObject.getSprite());
}
```

In this example, the GraphicsRenderer class encapsulates the rendering functionality. It relies on an SFML RenderWindow for rendering and provides a method for rendering game objects. This module has a single responsibility—graphics rendering—and is encapsulated to prevent direct access to the window.

Conclusion

Designing modular components in SFML-based projects is a fundamental practice for creating maintainable and extensible code. By following principles such as SRP, encapsulation, dependency management, and customization, you can build a modular architecture that promotes code reusability, ease of maintenance, collaboration, and scalability. Whether you're developing a small application or a complex game, modular design will enhance your project's structure and maintainability.

Section 7.3: Creating Custom Interfaces and APIs

In the context of developing applications and games with SFML, creating custom interfaces and APIs is a powerful technique for achieving modularity and flexibility. Custom interfaces allow you to define clear contracts between different parts of your code, enabling seamless integration of modules and promoting code reusability. In this section, we'll delve into the process of creating custom interfaces and APIs within SFML-based projects.

What Are Custom Interfaces and APIs?

Custom interfaces and APIs (Application Programming Interfaces) are well-defined sets of functions, methods, and data structures that allow different parts of your code to interact with each other in a standardized way. In the context of SFML development, custom interfaces and APIs serve the following purposes:

1. **Abstraction:** They abstract the underlying implementation details, allowing modules to interact at a high level without needing to understand each other's inner workings.

2. **Isolation:** They provide isolation between different modules, reducing the risk of unintended interactions or dependencies.

3. **Flexibility:** They offer flexibility by defining a clear contract. Modules that adhere to this contract can be easily swapped or extended without affecting the overall system.

Creating Custom Interfaces

Creating custom interfaces typically involves defining abstract classes or interfaces that specify a set of methods and properties that derived classes must implement. These interfaces act as contracts, ensuring that any class that implements them adheres to a specific behavior.

For example, in an SFML-based game development project, you might create a custom input interface:

```
// InputInterface.hpp

class InputInterface {
public:
    virtual bool IsKeyPressed(sf::Keyboard::Key key) = 0;
    virtual sf::Vector2f GetMousePosition() = 0;
    virtual ~InputInterface() = default;
};
```

In this example, InputInterface is an abstract class with two pure virtual methods (IsKeyPressed and GetMousePosition). Any class that wants to provide input functionality must implement these methods.

Implementing Custom APIs

Custom APIs define a set of functions or methods that provide a specific functionality to the rest of the codebase. They encapsulate complex operations and present a simplified, high-level interface.

For instance, in an SFML-based graphics rendering module, you might create a custom API for rendering game objects:

```cpp
// GraphicsAPI.hpp

class GraphicsAPI {
public:
    static void Initialize(sf::RenderWindow& window);
    static void RenderGameObject(const GameObject& gameObject);
    static void Clear();
    static void Display();
};
```

In this case, the GraphicsAPI class provides static methods for initializing rendering, rendering game objects, clearing the screen, and displaying the rendered content. These methods abstract the details of SFML rendering and provide a straightforward interface for other modules to use.

Advantages of Custom Interfaces and APIs

Custom interfaces and APIs offer several advantages in SFML-based projects:

1. **Decoupling:** They decouple modules, reducing dependencies and making the codebase more modular.

2. **Testing:** They facilitate unit testing by allowing you to create mock implementations of interfaces for testing specific modules independently.

3. **Extensibility:** They make it easier to extend or replace modules without affecting the rest of the code.

4. **Code Organization:** They enhance code organization by providing clear contracts and encapsulating complex functionality.

Conclusion

Creating custom interfaces and APIs is a valuable technique for achieving modularity and flexibility in SFML-based projects. Whether you're designing input systems, graphics rendering, audio playback, or other components, custom interfaces and APIs help define clear contracts and abstract implementation details, promoting code reusability and maintainability. By adopting this approach, you can create a more structured and extensible codebase, which is essential for developing scalable and maintainable applications and games.

Section 7.4: Implementing Plug-and-Play Functionality

Implementing plug-and-play functionality is a crucial aspect of modular development in SFML-based projects. This approach allows you to dynamically load and integrate external modules or extensions into your application or game, enhancing its functionality without the need for extensive code modifications. In this section, we'll explore how to implement plug-and-play functionality effectively.

Understanding Plug-and-Play

Plug-and-play, often referred to as "dynamic loading" or "runtime extension," is a concept where external modules or plugins can be added to an application at runtime, expanding its capabilities without requiring a recompilation of the main program. This approach offers several advantages:

1. **Scalability:** You can add new features or functionality to your application without altering its core codebase.

2. **Customization:** Users or developers can create and integrate their own plugins, tailoring the application to their specific needs.

3. **Maintainability:** It simplifies the process of maintaining and updating individual plugins independently.

Dynamic Loading in C++

In C++, dynamic loading of external libraries or plugins can be achieved using the `dlopen` and `dlsym` functions on Unix-like systems (Linux, macOS) or `LoadLibrary` and `GetProcAddress` functions on Windows. However, for cross-platform compatibility, you can use libraries like "libdl" on Unix-like systems and "LoadLibrary" on Windows via conditional compilation.

Here's a simplified example of dynamic loading in C++:

```cpp
#include <iostream>
#include <dlfcn.h>

int main() {
    void* pluginHandle = dlopen("my_plugin.so", RTLD_LAZY);  // Load the plug
in
    if (!pluginHandle) {
        std::cerr << "Error loading plugin: " << dlerror() << std::endl;
        return 1;
    }

    // Get a function pointer from the loaded plugin
    void (*pluginFunction)() = (void (*)())dlsym(pluginHandle, "MyPluginFunct
ion");
```

```
    if (!pluginFunction) {
        std::cerr << "Error finding function in plugin: " << dlerror() << std
::endl;
        dlclose(pluginHandle);   // Unload the plugin
        return 1;
    }

    // Call the function from the plugin
    pluginFunction();

    dlclose(pluginHandle);   // Unload the plugin

    return 0;
}
```

In this example, we load a dynamic library ("my_plugin.so") at runtime, obtain a function pointer to a function within the library, and then call that function.

To implement plug-and-play functionality in an SFML-based project, you can create a plugin system that dynamically loads external modules or extensions, such as additional game levels, custom input handlers, or new rendering effects. Here are the general steps to follow:

1. Define a clear plugin interface: Create an interface or set of conventions that external modules must adhere to, specifying the functions or methods they should implement.

2. Implement a dynamic loading mechanism: Use platform-specific dynamic loading functions (e.g., dlopen/dlsym or LoadLibrary/GetProcAddress) or cross-platform libraries (e.g., libdl) to load external modules at runtime.

3. Load and manage plugins: Design a system that can discover, load, and manage available plugins. This could involve searching specific directories for plugin files or using configuration files to define which plugins to load.

4. Integration with the main application: Once loaded, integrate the functionality provided by the plugins into the main application, whether it's extending the game logic, adding new menu options, or enhancing rendering.

Implementing plug-and-play functionality in SFML-based projects allows for dynamic extensibility and customization of your applications and games. By following best practices for dynamic loading, defining clear plugin interfaces, and managing the integration of external modules, you can create versatile and modular applications that can evolve and adapt to changing requirements without the need for extensive code modifications. This approach enhances code maintainability and fosters a more flexible and collaborative development process.

Section 7.5: Building Extensible Multimedia Applications

Building extensible multimedia applications is a goal that many software developers aspire to achieve. Extensibility enables your application to evolve and grow by allowing third-party developers to create plugins, extensions, or custom modules that enhance its capabilities. In this section, we will explore the concepts and techniques behind building extensible multimedia applications using SFML.

The Importance of Extensibility

Extensibility is crucial in the context of multimedia applications for several reasons:

1. **Customization:** It enables users to customize the application to their specific needs, enhancing their overall experience.

2. **Scalability:** As your application's user base grows, extensibility allows you to add new features and functionality without major code changes.

3. **Community Involvement:** Extensible applications attract a community of developers who can contribute plugins and extensions, fostering collaboration and innovation.

Designing an Extensible Architecture

To build an extensible multimedia application with SFML, consider the following design principles:

1. **Plugin System:** Implement a robust plugin system that allows external modules to be dynamically loaded and integrated into the application.

2. **Clear Interfaces:** Define clear and well-documented interfaces for plugins, specifying the methods or hooks that plugins must provide.

3. **Event System:** Create an event-driven architecture that enables plugins to subscribe to events and respond to various application events, such as user interactions or state changes.

4. **Configuration:** Implement a configuration system that allows users to specify which plugins should be loaded and their settings.

Creating a Plugin System

A plugin system in SFML typically involves dynamic loading of shared libraries (DLLs or shared objects) that contain the plugin's code. Here's a simplified example of how to load and manage plugins in C++:

```cpp
#include <iostream>
#include <vector>
#include <string>
#include <dlfcn.h> // On Unix-like systems
// #include <windows.h> // On Windows

class Plugin {
public:
    virtual void Initialize() = 0;
    virtual void Execute() = 0;
    virtual void Shutdown() = 0;
};

int main() {
    std::vector<Plugin*> plugins;

    // Load plugins from a directory or configuration file
    LoadPlugins(plugins);

    // Initialize and execute loaded plugins
    for (Plugin* plugin : plugins) {
        plugin->Initialize();
        plugin->Execute();
    }

    // Clean up and unload plugins
    for (Plugin* plugin : plugins) {
        plugin->Shutdown();
        delete plugin;
    }

    return 0;
}
```

In this example, we define a Plugin interface and load plugins dynamically. Each loaded plugin is initialized, executed, and shut down as needed.

Managing Plugins in SFML

SFML provides the foundation for building extensible multimedia applications. You can use SFML for graphics rendering, audio playback, and user interaction while designing a plugin system to extend its functionality. Here are some ways to manage plugins in SFML-based applications:

1. **Graphics Plugins:** Create plugins that add custom rendering effects, post-processing, or new graphical elements to your application.

2. **Audio Plugins:** Extend the audio capabilities of your application by allowing plugins to provide custom audio processing or synthesis.

3. **Input Plugins:** Enable plugins to define custom input handling or support additional input devices.

4. **UI Plugins:** Build a user interface system that allows plugins to contribute custom UI components or widgets.

5. **Game Logic Plugins:** Implement game logic plugins that define new game rules, levels, or AI behaviors.

6. **Extensions:** Develop extensions for multimedia editing applications that provide new features like filters, animations, or transitions.

Conclusion

Building extensible multimedia applications with SFML opens up a world of possibilities for customization and growth. By designing a flexible architecture, implementing a robust plugin system, and providing clear interfaces for plugins, you can create applications that continue to evolve and meet the diverse needs of your user base. Extensibility encourages community involvement and fosters innovation, making your multimedia application a dynamic and vibrant platform.

Chapter 8: Building a Cross-Platform Drawing Application

Section 8.1: Designing a Drawing Application Project

In this section, we'll delve into the process of designing a cross-platform drawing application using SFML. A drawing application allows users to create, edit, and manipulate digital artwork, making it a versatile tool for artists, designers, and anyone interested in expressing their creativity digitally.

Understanding the Drawing Application

Before diving into the technical details, it's essential to have a clear understanding of what a drawing application should offer. Here are some fundamental features you might consider:

1. **Canvas:** The core of the application, where users create and edit their artwork. It should support various drawing tools, such as pencils, brushes, shapes, and text.

2. **Layers:** Support for multiple layers enables users to organize their artwork efficiently. Each layer can have its properties, such as opacity and blending modes.

3. **Undo and Redo:** Users should be able to undo and redo their actions, providing a safety net for creative experimentation.

4. **File Management:** The ability to save and load drawings in different formats, such as PNG, JPEG, or the application's custom format.

5. **User Interface:** A user-friendly interface with tools, color palettes, and options accessible via menus or panels.

6. **Customization:** Allow users to customize the application's appearance, hotkeys, and tool settings.

Planning the Application Architecture

Designing a drawing application requires careful planning of the software architecture. Here are some architectural considerations:

1. **MVC (Model-View-Controller):** Divide the application into separate components for handling data (model), user interface (view), and user interactions (controller).

2. **Graphics Rendering:** Use SFML for rendering graphics and managing the graphical user interface. SFML provides robust support for 2D graphics, which is suitable for a drawing application.

3. **Event Handling:** Implement event handlers to capture user input, such as mouse clicks, keyboard input, and stylus interactions.

4. **Undo/Redo Stack:** Create a stack to store the application's states, allowing users to navigate backward and forward through their actions.

5. **Layer Management:** Develop a system for managing layers, including the ability to reorder, merge, and delete layers.

6. **File I/O:** Integrate file I/O functionality to save and load drawings in various formats.

7. **Toolset:** Implement a toolset that includes brushes, pencils, erasers, shapes, and text tools. Each tool should have customizable settings.

Cross-Platform Considerations

Since our goal is to create a cross-platform drawing application, we need to consider platform-specific differences and requirements. SFML simplifies many cross-platform challenges, but you should still be aware of the following:

1. **File Paths:** Handle file paths and file dialogs in a way that works seamlessly on different operating systems.

2. **Window Management:** Ensure that window management and screen resolution adjustments are handled appropriately for various platforms.

3. **Input Devices:** Support different input devices, such as mice, touchscreens, and graphics tablets, while providing a consistent user experience.

4. **UI Scaling:** Address differences in screen sizes and DPI settings to ensure the application looks and works well on all devices.

In the next sections, we will explore specific aspects of implementing a cross-platform drawing application, including user input handling, advanced drawing tools, managing layers, and exporting artwork for use across different platforms.

Section 8.2: Handling User Input for Drawing and Editing

In a drawing application, effective handling of user input is essential to provide a smooth and intuitive drawing experience. This section will explore how to manage user input for drawing and editing operations in a cross-platform SFML-based drawing application.

Mouse Input Handling

Mouse input is a primary means of interaction in a drawing application. SFML provides straightforward ways to capture mouse events, such as clicks, movement, and button presses. Here's a basic example of handling mouse input in SFML:

```
sf::RenderWindow window(sf::VideoMode(800, 600), "Drawing App");
```

```cpp
while (window.isOpen()) {
    sf::Event event;
    while (window.pollEvent(event)) {
        if (event.type == sf::Event::Closed) {
            window.close();
        }
        else if (event.type == sf::Event::MouseButtonPressed) {
            if (event.mouseButton.button == sf::Mouse::Left) {
                // Handle left mouse button click (start drawing)
            }
            else if (event.mouseButton.button == sf::Mouse::Right) {
                // Handle right mouse button click (context menu or other act
ions)
            }
        }
        else if (event.type == sf::Event::MouseButtonReleased) {
            if (event.mouseButton.button == sf::Mouse::Left) {
                // Handle left mouse button release (stop drawing)
            }
        }
        else if (event.type == sf::Event::MouseMoved) {
            // Handle mouse movement (update drawing position)
        }
    }

    // Drawing and rendering logic here
    // ...
}
```

In this example, we detect mouse button presses, releases, and movement to initiate and stop drawing actions and update the drawing position.

Touch Input Handling

For touchscreen devices, it's essential to support touch input, making your application more versatile. SFML simplifies touch input handling with a similar approach to mouse input:

```cpp
sf::RenderWindow window(sf::VideoMode(800, 600), "Drawing App");

while (window.isOpen()) {
    sf::Event event;
    while (window.pollEvent(event)) {
        if (event.type == sf::Event::Closed) {
            window.close();
        }
        else if (event.type == sf::Event::TouchBegan) {
            // Handle touch input (e.g., start drawing)
        }
        else if (event.type == sf::Event::TouchMoved) {
```

```
            // Handle touch movement (e.g., update drawing position)
        }
        else if (event.type == sf::Event::TouchEnded) {
            // Handle touch release (e.g., stop drawing)
        }
    }

    // Drawing and rendering logic here
    // ...
}
```

By detecting touch events, you can provide a touch-friendly interface for users on devices like smartphones and tablets.

Stylus Input

Graphics tablets and stylus pens offer precise input for drawing applications. SFML can also capture stylus input events, allowing users to create detailed and accurate artwork:

```
sf::RenderWindow window(sf::VideoMode(800, 600), "Drawing App");

while (window.isOpen()) {
    sf::Event event;
    while (window.pollEvent(event)) {
        if (event.type == sf::Event::Closed) {
            window.close();
        }
        else if (event.type == sf::Event::TabletPressed) {
            // Handle stylus press (e.g., start drawing)
        }
        else if (event.type == sf::Event::TabletReleased) {
            // Handle stylus release (e.g., stop drawing)
        }
        else if (event.type == sf::Event::TabletMoved) {
            // Handle stylus movement (e.g., update drawing position)
        }
    }

    // Drawing and rendering logic here
    // ...
}
```

Incorporating stylus input support ensures that your drawing application caters to the needs of professional artists and designers who rely on high-precision input devices.

In the following sections, we will explore advanced drawing tools and techniques to enhance the drawing capabilities of your cross-platform application further.

Section 8.3: Implementing Advanced Drawing Tools

In a drawing application, providing users with a variety of drawing tools and options is crucial for unleashing their creativity. This section focuses on implementing advanced drawing tools to enhance the functionality of your cross-platform SFML-based drawing application.

Brush and Pen Options

Brushes and pens are fundamental drawing tools. You can implement different brush shapes, sizes, and colors to offer users a wide range of creative possibilities. SFML's graphics capabilities make it easy to implement these features:

```cpp
sf::RenderWindow window(sf::VideoMode(800, 600), "Drawing App");
sf::RenderTexture canvas;
canvas.create(800, 600);

sf::CircleShape brush;
brush.setRadius(10); // Set the brush size
brush.setFillColor(sf::Color::Black); // Set the brush color

while (window.isOpen()) {
    sf::Event event;
    while (window.pollEvent(event)) {
        if (event.type == sf::Event::Closed) {
            window.close();
        }
        else if (event.type == sf::Event::MouseButtonPressed && event.mouseBu
tton.button == sf::Mouse::Left) {
            // Draw with the selected brush at the mouse position
            brush.setPosition(sf::Vector2f(event.mouseButton.x, event.mouseBu
tton.y));
            canvas.draw(brush);
            canvas.display();
        }
    }

    // Render the canvas
    sf::Sprite canvasSprite(canvas.getTexture());
    window.clear();
    window.draw(canvasSprite);
    window.display();
}
```

In this example, we create a brush using an SFML `CircleShape` and use it to draw on a render texture. Users can change the brush size, color, and shape to create a variety of strokes.

Line and Shape Tools

Enhance your drawing application by adding tools for drawing lines and shapes like rectangles, circles, and polygons. These tools provide users with more structured drawing options:

```cpp
sf::RenderWindow window(sf::VideoMode(800, 600), "Drawing App");
sf::RenderTexture canvas;
canvas.create(800, 600);

bool drawingLine = false;
sf::VertexArray currentLine(sf::LinesStrip, 0);
sf::RectangleShape rectangle;
// Initialize other shape variables

while (window.isOpen()) {
    sf::Event event;
    while (window.pollEvent(event)) {
        if (event.type == sf::Event::Closed) {
            window.close();
        }
        else if (event.type == sf::Event::MouseButtonPressed && event.mouseButton.button == sf::Mouse::Left) {
            // Handle shape or line tool activation
            if (/* User selects line tool */) {
                drawingLine = true;
                currentLine.clear();
            }
            else if (/* User selects rectangle tool */) {
                // Initialize rectangle drawing
            }
            // Handle other shape tools similarly
        }
        else if (event.type == sf::Event::MouseButtonReleased && event.mouseButton.button == sf::Mouse::Left) {
            // Finish drawing the current shape or line
            if (drawingLine) {
                // Store the drawn line
            }
            else if (/* Drawing a rectangle */) {
                // Finish drawing the rectangle
            }
            // Handle other shapes
        }
        else if (event.type == sf::Event::MouseMoved) {
            // Update the shape or line being drawn
            if (drawingLine) {
                currentLine.append(sf::Vertex(sf::Vector2f(event.mouseMove.x, event.mouseMove.y)));
            }
```

```
        else if (/* Drawing a rectangle */) {
            // Update rectangle dimensions
        }
        // Handle other shapes
    }
}

// Drawing and rendering logic here
// ...
}
```

By adding line and shape tools, your application becomes versatile, allowing users to create both freehand and structured drawings.

Eraser and Undo

Mistakes happen, so it's essential to include an eraser tool and undo functionality in your drawing application. Users can easily correct errors and experiment without fear of losing their work:

```
// Inside the event loop
else if (event.type == sf::Event::KeyPressed) {
    if (event.key.code == sf::Keyboard::E) {
        // Activate the eraser tool
        brush.setFillColor(sf::Color::White); // Set the brush color to white
for erasing
    }
    else if (event.key.code == sf::Keyboard::Z && event.key.control) {
        // Implement undo functionality
        // Pop the last drawing action or clear the canvas
    }
}
else if (event.type == sf::Event::KeyReleased) {
    if (event.key.code == sf::Keyboard::E) {
        // Deactivate the eraser tool
        brush.setFillColor(sf::Color::Black); // Reset the brush color to bla
ck
    }
}
```

By toggling the brush color between black and white, you can switch between drawing and erasing modes. Additionally, implementing an undo feature allows users to revert to previous states of their artwork.

Incorporating these advanced drawing tools not only enhances your application's functionality but also provides users with a more comprehensive drawing experience, making your cross-platform SFML-based drawing application a powerful creative tool.

Section 8.4: Managing Layers and Customization Options

In a cross-platform drawing application, providing users with the ability to work on multiple layers and customize their drawing experience can greatly enhance their creative process. This section focuses on managing layers and offering customization options within your SFML-based drawing application.

Layer Management

Implementing layers allows users to separate different elements of their artwork and work on them independently. You can create a layer system that enables users to add, remove, reorder, and toggle the visibility of layers:

```cpp
std::vector<sf::RenderTexture> layers; // Vector to store layers
sf::RenderTexture currentLayer; // The layer currently being drawn on
int activeLayerIndex = 0; // Index of the currently active layer

// Function to add a new layer
void addLayer() {
    sf::RenderTexture newLayer;
    newLayer.create(800, 600);
    layers.push_back(newLayer);
}

// Function to switch between layers
void setActiveLayer(int layerIndex) {
    if (layerIndex >= 0 && layerIndex < layers.size()) {
        activeLayerIndex = layerIndex;
        currentLayer = layers[layerIndex];
    }
}

// Function to draw on the current active layer
void drawOnActiveLayer(sf::Drawable& drawable) {
    currentLayer.draw(drawable);
    currentLayer.display();
}

// Function to render all layers onto the canvas
void renderLayers(sf::RenderWindow& window) {
    window.clear();
    for (int i = 0; i < layers.size(); ++i) {
        sf::Sprite layerSprite(layers[i].getTexture());
        window.draw(layerSprite);
    }
    window.display();
}
```

With this layer management system, users can create complex artwork by drawing on separate layers and controlling their visibility as needed.

Customization Options

Offering customization options allows users to tailor their drawing experience. You can provide features like color selection, brush size adjustment, and opacity control:

```cpp
sf::Color selectedColor = sf::Color::Black; // Default color
int brushSize = 10; // Default brush size
int opacity = 255; // Default opacity (fully opaque)

// Function to change the brush color
void changeColor(sf::Color newColor) {
    selectedColor = newColor;
    brush.setFillColor(selectedColor);
}

// Function to adjust the brush size
void changeBrushSize(int newSize) {
    brushSize = newSize;
    brush.setRadius(static_cast<float>(brushSize));
}

// Function to change the opacity
void changeOpacity(int newOpacity) {
    opacity = newOpacity;
    // Modify the opacity of the brush or other drawing tools
    brush.setFillColor(sf::Color(selectedColor.r, selectedColor.g, selectedColor.b, opacity));
}
```

By providing customization options, users can express their creativity and achieve the desired effects in their artwork.

User-Friendly Interface

To make these features accessible, create a user-friendly interface with buttons, sliders, or a menu system that allows users to interact with layer management and customization options easily.

Incorporating layer management and customization options into your SFML-based drawing application empowers users to create intricate and personalized artwork while enjoying a seamless cross-platform experience.

Section 8.5: Exporting and Sharing Artwork Across Platforms

Allowing users to export and share their artwork is a crucial feature for a cross-platform drawing application. In this section, we'll explore methods to implement this functionality, ensuring that users can easily save and share their creations.

File Export Options

Provide users with various file export options, such as saving their artwork in different formats like PNG, JPEG, or even vector formats like SVG. To do this, you can use SFML's built-in image saving capabilities:

```cpp
sf::Image screenshot = window.capture(); // Capture the current canvas
screenshot.saveToFile("artwork.png"); // Save as PNG
```

For more format options, you might consider integrating third-party libraries like `libpng` or `libjpeg` to support additional file types.

Cloud Storage Integration

To enable seamless sharing across platforms, consider integrating cloud storage services like Dropbox, Google Drive, or OneDrive. Allow users to authenticate and upload their artwork directly to their chosen cloud storage accounts. You can use APIs provided by these services for integration.

```cpp
// Pseudocode for uploading to Dropbox
void uploadToDropbox(sf::Image& artwork) {
    DropboxAPI.authenticate();
    DropboxAPI.uploadFile("artwork.png", artwork);
}
```

Social Media Sharing

Integrating social media sharing features can also enhance the user experience. Allow users to share their artwork on platforms like Facebook, Twitter, or Instagram with a single click. Utilize the social media platforms' APIs to facilitate this sharing:

```cpp
// Pseudocode for sharing on Twitter
void shareOnTwitter(sf::Image& artwork) {
    TwitterAPI.authenticate();
    TwitterAPI.shareImage("Check out my artwork!", artwork);
}
```

Cross-Platform Compatibility

Ensure that the exported files are compatible with various devices and platforms. Consider implementing automatic file format conversion if needed to guarantee that users can open their artwork on different devices without compatibility issues.

Create an intuitive export and sharing interface within your application. This can include options for selecting the export format, choosing the destination (local storage, cloud storage, social media), and adding descriptions or hashtags for social media posts.

By implementing these export and sharing features, your cross-platform drawing application becomes a versatile tool for artists and creators to save, share, and showcase their artwork across different platforms and devices.

Chapter 9: Audio Synthesis and Real-Time Processing

Section 9.1: Understanding Audio Synthesis Concepts

Audio synthesis is the process of generating sound waveforms electronically. It's a fundamental concept in multimedia programming, especially in applications that require creating or modifying audio in real-time. This section introduces you to the essential concepts of audio synthesis and provides insights into how it can be used in your projects.

Sound as Waveforms

Sound in its most basic form can be represented as a waveform. A waveform is a visual representation of a sound's amplitude (loudness) over time. Common waveforms include sine waves, square waves, sawtooth waves, and triangle waves. Each waveform has a unique timbre or tonal quality.

Sine Wave

A sine wave is the simplest waveform and consists of a single frequency with no harmonics. It produces a pure, smooth tone.

```cpp
// Generating a sine wave in C++
float frequency = 440.0; // Frequency in Hertz (Hz)
float amplitude = 0.5; // Amplitude (volume)
float sampleRate = 44100.0; // Sample rate in samples per second (Hz)
float duration = 2.0; // Duration in seconds

sf::SoundBuffer buffer;
sf::Int16* samples = new sf::Int16[int(sampleRate * duration)];

for (int i = 0; i < int(sampleRate * duration); i++) {
    samples[i] = amplitude * 32767.0 * std::sin(2.0 * 3.14159265 * frequency
* i / sampleRate);
}

buffer.loadFromSamples(samples, int(sampleRate * duration), 2, int(sampleRate
));
sf::Sound sound(buffer);
sound.play();
```

Other Waveforms

Other waveforms can be generated similarly by changing the waveform function (e.g., square, sawtooth) used in the above code.

Envelopes are used to shape the amplitude of a sound over time, allowing you to create dynamic and expressive sounds. The most common envelope parameters are Attack, Decay, Sustain, and Release (ADSR).

- **Attack**: The time it takes for the sound to reach its maximum amplitude from zero when a note is played.
- **Decay**: The time it takes for the sound to decrease from the maximum amplitude to the sustain level.
- **Sustain**: The level at which the sound remains as long as the note is held.
- **Release**: The time it takes for the sound to fade out when the note is released.

By controlling these parameters, you can simulate a wide range of natural and synthetic sounds.

Frequency Modulation (FM)

Frequency modulation is a technique where the frequency of one waveform (the carrier) is modulated by another waveform (the modulator). This creates complex, evolving timbres and is commonly used in synthesizers.

Granular Synthesis

Granular synthesis involves breaking sound into tiny grains and manipulating them individually. This technique allows for granular control over sound textures and is often used in sound design and experimental music.

Understanding these audio synthesis concepts is essential for creating custom audio effects, interactive music, and real-time audio processing in multimedia applications. You can use these techniques to generate and manipulate sound dynamically, adding depth and richness to your projects.

Section 9.2: Implementing Real-Time Audio Processing

Real-time audio processing is a crucial aspect of multimedia programming, enabling applications to manipulate and modify audio data as it's being played or recorded. In this section, we'll explore the fundamental concepts and techniques for implementing real-time audio processing in your projects.

Audio Buffers and Sample Rates

Audio data is typically processed in discrete chunks known as audio buffers. These buffers contain a fixed number of audio samples, and the sample rate determines how many samples are processed per second. Common sample rates include 44.1 kHz and 48 kHz, but other rates are used in various contexts.

When working with real-time audio processing, you'll often deal with circular audio buffers that continuously fill and empty as audio data is captured or played. This allows for seamless processing without interruption.

Digital Signal Processing (DSP)

DSP techniques are at the core of real-time audio processing. DSP involves applying mathematical operations to audio samples to modify their characteristics. Some common DSP operations include filtering, convolution, pitch shifting, time stretching, and applying audio effects like reverb or equalization.

Here's an example of applying a simple low-pass filter in real-time using a circular buffer:

```
// Pseudocode for a low-pass filter
for each audio buffer:
    for each sample in the buffer:
        current_sample = input_buffer[sample_index];
        filtered_sample = (1.0 - alpha) * current_sample + alpha * previous_sample;
        previous_sample = filtered_sample;
        output_buffer[sample_index] = filtered_sample;
```

In this code, alpha controls the cutoff frequency of the filter. Smaller values of alpha result in a lower cutoff frequency, allowing only low-frequency components to pass through.

Latency

Real-time audio processing introduces a challenge known as latency. Latency is the delay between capturing or receiving audio data and producing the processed output. High latency can lead to perceptible delays between user actions and audio feedback, negatively impacting the user experience.

To minimize latency, you can employ techniques like buffer size optimization, multithreading, and audio hardware configuration. Reducing latency is critical for applications such as audio recording, live music performance, and real-time audio effects.

Audio Effects and Plugins

Real-time audio processing often involves applying audio effects in real-time. These effects can include reverb, chorus, delay, and distortion, among others. To implement audio effects, you can create audio effect plugins that can be dynamically loaded into your audio processing pipeline. These plugins process the audio data as it flows through the pipeline.

Real-Time Synthesis

Real-time audio processing is also used for real-time audio synthesis. This allows you to generate sound dynamically, which is useful for music synthesis, interactive applications, and games. You can create synthesizers that produce complex sounds in response to user input or other events.

Understanding real-time audio processing is essential for multimedia developers working on applications that require audio manipulation, synthesis, or effects. Whether you're building music software, games, or interactive multimedia installations, real-time audio processing opens up a world of creative possibilities.

Section 9.3: Creating Custom Audio Effects

Creating custom audio effects is a fascinating aspect of audio programming that allows you to apply unique and tailored modifications to audio signals. In this section, we will delve into the process of designing and implementing custom audio effects for your multimedia applications.

Understanding Audio Effects

Audio effects alter the characteristics of an audio signal to achieve specific sonic qualities. They can range from simple adjustments like equalization and filtering to more complex transformations like modulation, time-based effects, and convolution. Understanding the principles behind audio effects is crucial before diving into custom effect development.

Effect Design and Parameters

To create custom audio effects, you first need to design the effect and define its parameters. Parameters are the adjustable settings that control the effect's behavior. For instance, in a reverb effect, parameters might include the room size, decay time, and wet/dry mix. Your goal is to determine how these parameters will affect the audio signal.

Here's a simplified example of designing a custom audio effect—a tremolo effect:

```
// Pseudocode for a basic tremolo effect
for each audio buffer:
    for each sample in the buffer:
        // Calculate the tremolo gain based on an LFO (Low-Frequency Oscillator)
        tremolo_gain = (1.0 + depth * sin(2 * pi * frequency * time));
        // Apply the tremolo gain to the audio sample
        output_sample = input_sample * tremolo_gain;
    end for
end for
```

In this example, the effect's parameters include depth (intensity) and frequency (speed of the tremolo).

Real-Time Implementation

Most audio effects are implemented in real-time, meaning they process audio data as it's being played or recorded. This requires efficient and low-latency algorithms to ensure a seamless audio experience for users.

Real-time implementation often involves circular audio buffers, where incoming audio is continuously processed, and the processed audio is streamed to the output. Optimizing the algorithm and minimizing latency are critical aspects of creating effective custom audio effects.

Audio Effect Plugins

Audio effect plugins are a common way to integrate custom audio effects into digital audio workstations (DAWs) or other audio processing software. These plugins are dynamically loaded and applied to audio tracks. Popular audio plugin formats include VST, Audio Unit, and AAX.

Developing audio effect plugins typically involves adhering to a specific plugin standard, such as the VST SDK, and implementing the audio effect logic within the plugin. This allows users to apply your custom effects within their preferred audio software.

Real-World Applications

Custom audio effects are used in a wide range of applications, including music production, live sound engineering, and multimedia software development. Musicians and sound designers often use them to shape the timbre and character of sound recordings, while multimedia developers utilize them to enhance the audio experience in games, virtual reality, and interactive installations.

By mastering the art of creating custom audio effects, you can add a unique sonic signature to your multimedia projects and provide users with immersive and captivating audio experiences. Whether it's crafting innovative soundscapes or fine-tuning audio for multimedia applications, custom audio effects play a pivotal role in modern audio production and multimedia development.

Section 9.4: Interactive Music Generation with SFML

Interactive music generation is an exciting field that allows you to create dynamic and adaptive soundtracks for multimedia applications, games, and interactive experiences. In this section, we will explore how to implement interactive music generation using the Simple and Fast Multimedia Library (SFML) and other related tools and techniques.

The Role of Interactive Music

Traditional linear music compositions follow a predefined structure, playing the same melody and arrangement each time they are heard. In contrast, interactive music adapts to the user's actions or the context of the application, providing a more immersive and engaging experience. Interactive music can respond to in-game events, changes in gameplay, or user input, making it an essential element in modern multimedia applications.

Interactive music generation involves several key concepts:

1. **Music Layers**: Interactive music often consists of multiple layers or tracks that can be independently controlled. Each layer may represent different instruments, melodies, or soundscapes.

2. **Sequencing**: The sequencing of music elements (e.g., notes, chords, percussion) is essential. Sequences can be predefined or generated algorithmically in real-time.

3. **States and Transitions**: The application's states and transitions trigger changes in the music. For example, transitioning from exploration to combat in a game can trigger a change in the music's intensity.

4. **Dynamic Mixing**: Interactive music may involve real-time mixing of audio elements to create a cohesive and adaptive soundtrack. This requires controlling the volume, panning, and effects of individual layers.

Implementing Interactive Music with SFML

SFML provides a foundation for interactive music generation by offering audio playback and sound manipulation capabilities. To implement interactive music, follow these steps:

1. **Design the Music Layers**: Determine the layers or tracks that make up your interactive music. For instance, you might have separate layers for background ambiance, melodies, and percussion.

2. **Sequencing and State Management**: Create sequences for each layer and define how they change based on the application's states and events. SFML's event handling can be used to trigger state changes.

3. **Real-Time Control**: Use SFML's audio features to control playback, volume, and other audio properties in real-time. You can manipulate audio buffers and streams to achieve dynamic mixing.

4. **Integration with Game Logic**: If you're developing a game, integrate the interactive music system with your game's logic. Ensure that gameplay events trigger appropriate changes in the music.

5. **User Feedback and Testing**: Continuously test your interactive music system to ensure it responds appropriately to user interactions. Solicit feedback to refine the music's adaptive qualities.

Here's a simplified example of how you might implement interactive music generation in an SFML-based game:

```
// Pseudocode for interactive music in a game
while (window.isOpen()) {
    // Handle user input and game events
```

```
handleEvents();

// Determine the current game state
GameState currentState = determineState();

// Update the music based on the game state
updateMusic(currentState);

// Render the game
render();
}
```

Interactive music generation adds a layer of depth and engagement to multimedia applications. It allows you to create soundtracks that seamlessly adapt to the user's actions or the context of the application, enhancing the overall user experience. By mastering the principles of interactive music, you can create memorable and immersive audio environments in your projects.

Section 9.5: Performance Optimization for Real-Time Audio

Optimizing the performance of real-time audio processing is crucial to ensure that audio applications, games, or multimedia projects run smoothly and provide a seamless experience for users. In this section, we will explore various techniques and considerations for optimizing the performance of real-time audio in applications built with the Simple and Fast Multimedia Library (SFML) or similar frameworks.

Understanding Real-Time Audio Constraints

Real-time audio processing involves generating or manipulating audio data in a way that allows for immediate playback with minimal delay. This is critical for applications that require synchronized audio, such as games, music software, and interactive multimedia. Here are some key constraints and challenges in real-time audio:

1. **Low Latency**: Real-time audio processing must minimize latency, which is the delay between an action (e.g., pressing a key, firing a gun) and hearing the corresponding sound.

2. **Stable Frame Rates**: Consistent frame rates are essential to ensure that audio processing and rendering are synchronized with other aspects of an application, such as graphics.

3. **Efficient Memory Usage**: Audio data can be memory-intensive, so managing memory efficiently is crucial for preventing performance bottlenecks.

4. **Multi-Platform Considerations**: Ensuring that real-time audio works smoothly on different platforms and hardware configurations requires careful optimization.

To optimize real-time audio in SFML or similar libraries, consider the following techniques:

1. **Buffering and Preloading**: Preload audio data into memory and use buffering to minimize delays during playback. This ensures that audio data is readily available when needed.

2. **Streaming**: For large audio files or streams, use SFML's streaming capabilities to load and play audio progressively, reducing memory usage.

3. **Audio Compression**: Compress audio files to reduce their size without compromising quality. Popular formats like Ogg Vorbis and MP3 can be used for compressed audio.

4. **Thread Management**: Utilize separate threads for audio processing and rendering to avoid blocking the main application loop. Be mindful of thread synchronization to prevent data conflicts.

5. **Audio Resource Management**: Implement efficient resource management to load and unload audio assets as needed. This reduces memory overhead and improves overall performance.

6. **Sample Rate and Bit Depth**: Adjust the sample rate and bit depth of audio files to balance audio quality with performance. Lower values can reduce computational load.

7. **Effect Optimization**: Optimize audio effects and processing algorithms for efficiency. Use profiling tools to identify performance bottlenecks in effect processing.

8. **Platform-Specific Optimization**: Consider platform-specific optimizations, such as using platform-specific audio APIs or libraries when available.

9. **Profiling and Benchmarking**: Use profiling and benchmarking tools to identify performance bottlenecks and areas for improvement in your audio processing code.

10. **Testing on Target Hardware**: Test your audio code on the target hardware and configurations to ensure optimal performance across a range of devices.

Code Example: Multithreaded Audio Playback in SFML

```cpp
#include <SFML/Audio.hpp>
#include <SFML/System.hpp>

int main() {
    sf::RenderWindow window(sf::VideoMode(800, 600), "SFML Audio Example");

    // Create a thread for audio playback
    sf::Thread audioThread([&]() {
        sf::Music music;
```

```cpp
    if (!music.openFromFile("music.ogg")) {
        // Handle error
        return;
    }

    music.play();
});

audioThread.launch();

while (window.isOpen()) {
    sf::Event event;
    while (window.pollEvent(event)) {
        if (event.type == sf::Event::Closed) {
            window.close();
        }
    }

    window.clear();
    // Render your application's graphics here
    window.display();
}

return 0;
}
```

In this example, we create a separate thread for audio playback to avoid blocking the main application loop. This ensures that audio processing occurs independently, contributing to smoother real-time audio performance.

By carefully implementing these performance optimization techniques and considering the specific requirements of your application, you can achieve responsive and high-quality real-time audio playback in SFML-based projects.

Chapter 10: Game Development Frameworks on Top of SFML

Section 10.1: Overview of Game Development Frameworks

Game development frameworks are essential tools that streamline the process of creating games. They provide a foundation of pre-built functionality, tools, and systems to help game developers focus on game-specific features rather than reinventing the wheel. In this section, we'll explore an overview of game development frameworks that can be used in conjunction with SFML to accelerate game development.

The Role of Game Development Frameworks

Game development frameworks serve several important purposes:

1. **Abstraction of Low-Level Details**: Frameworks abstract low-level tasks like window management, input handling, and rendering, allowing developers to work at a higher level of abstraction.

2. **Efficient Asset Management**: Many frameworks offer asset management systems for handling graphics, audio, and other game assets.

3. **Physics Simulation**: Some frameworks include physics engines for simulating realistic object interactions and movements within the game world.

4. **Cross-Platform Support**: Frameworks often support multiple platforms, enabling developers to target a wide range of devices and operating systems.

5. **Community and Support**: Popular frameworks have active communities, which means access to tutorials, documentation, and a wealth of shared knowledge.

6. **Productivity Tools**: Frameworks may come with level editors, visual scripting tools, and debugging utilities to enhance developer productivity.

7. **Multiplayer Support**: Many frameworks include features for implementing multiplayer functionality, such as networking libraries and server integration.

Popular Game Development Frameworks

1. **Unity**: Unity is one of the most popular game development frameworks, known for its versatility and ease of use. It supports 2D and 3D game development and offers a visual editor for scene creation and scripting in C#.

2. **Unreal Engine**: Unreal Engine is renowned for its high-quality graphics and robust development tools. It uses the Blueprint visual scripting system and C++ for scripting.

3. **Godot Engine**: Godot is an open-source game engine that emphasizes flexibility and ease of use. It uses its own scripting language, GDScript, and provides a visual editor.

4. **Phaser**: Phaser is a JavaScript framework for 2D game development, making it accessible for web-based games. It's ideal for developers familiar with web technologies.

5. **LibGDX**: LibGDX is a Java-based framework suitable for 2D and 3D game development. It allows cross-platform development and is popular among indie developers.

6. **Love2D**: Love2D is an open-source framework for 2D game development using the Lua programming language. It's lightweight and great for prototyping.

7. **SFML Game Development**: While not a standalone framework, SFML can be used as the foundation for building custom game engines and frameworks, providing developers with flexibility and control over their projects.

Choosing the Right Framework

Selecting the right game development framework depends on your project's requirements, your team's expertise, and the platform(s) you want to target. Consider factors such as performance, community support, and the learning curve when making your decision. Ultimately, the chosen framework should align with your game's vision and development goals.

In the following sections, we will delve deeper into integrating some of these popular game development frameworks with SFML to create compelling and feature-rich games.

Section 10.2: Integrating Popular Frameworks with SFML

Integrating popular game development frameworks with SFML can open up a world of possibilities for game developers. These frameworks often come with built-in tools and libraries that complement SFML's capabilities. In this section, we'll explore how to integrate some of these popular frameworks with SFML to enhance your game development experience.

Unity Integration

Unity is a versatile game development framework known for its cross-platform support and ease of use. While Unity primarily uses C# for scripting, you can integrate it with SFML for specific use cases, such as incorporating custom rendering or leveraging SFML's multimedia features.

To integrate Unity with SFML:

1. Export your Unity project as a native application.
2. Use inter-process communication (IPC) mechanisms, such as sockets or shared memory, to exchange data between Unity and an SFML-based application. This

allows Unity to handle game logic while SFML handles specific tasks like rendering or audio.

Unreal Engine is renowned for its high-quality graphics and tools. Unreal uses C++ for scripting, and while it has its rendering engine, you can integrate SFML for additional rendering capabilities or to create 2D games within the Unreal environment.

To integrate Unreal Engine with SFML:

1. Create a new C++ project in Unreal Engine.
2. Use Unreal's built-in functions and classes to handle game logic and interactions.
3. Use SFML for rendering 2D elements or handling specific multimedia tasks.
4. Communication between Unreal and SFML can be achieved through function calls or shared data structures.

Godot Engine is known for its flexibility and ease of use. It uses GDScript (similar to Python) for scripting and provides a visual editor for creating game scenes. While Godot excels in 2D and 3D game development, you can integrate SFML for specific tasks like advanced 2D rendering or multimedia playback.

To integrate Godot Engine with SFML:

1. Create a new project in Godot Engine.
2. Develop the game logic and interactions using GDScript and Godot's visual scripting.
3. Use the Godot-SFML library or custom code to integrate SFML for rendering or multimedia features.
4. Ensure seamless communication between Godot and SFML components for a cohesive game experience.

Phaser is a JavaScript framework primarily used for web-based 2D game development. Integrating Phaser with SFML can be beneficial when you want to create both web and desktop versions of your game, sharing code and assets between the two platforms.

To integrate Phaser with SFML:

1. Develop the core game logic using Phaser's JavaScript-based framework.
2. Utilize the Electron framework to package your Phaser game as a desktop application.
3. Incorporate SFML for specific desktop-related features, such as handling window management or multimedia playback.
4. Ensure synchronization of game state between the Phaser and SFML components.

LibGDX is a Java-based framework suitable for 2D and 3D game development. Integrating LibGDX with SFML allows you to harness the power of Java for cross-platform game development and leverage SFML's multimedia capabilities.

To integrate LibGDX with SFML:

1. Create a LibGDX project using Java.
2. Use LibGDX's Scene2D for UI and game logic.
3. Integrate SFML through Java Native Interface (JNI) bindings or by using shared libraries.
4. Ensure proper synchronization and communication between LibGDX and SFML components.

Love2D is an open-source framework for 2D game development using the Lua programming language. Integrating Love2D with SFML can provide additional capabilities for rendering and multimedia handling in Love2D games.

To integrate Love2D with SFML:

1. Develop the game logic using Love2D's Lua-based framework.
2. Use Lua's C API to integrate SFML as a shared library.
3. Employ SFML for rendering, multimedia playback, or other specific features.
4. Ensure seamless communication and data exchange between Love2D and SFML components.

Incorporating these popular game development frameworks with SFML can help you leverage the strengths of both tools, enabling you to create more feature-rich and engaging games while benefiting from the ease of use and community support offered by these frameworks. The choice of integration depends on your project's specific requirements and your familiarity with the selected framework.

Section 10.3: Using Entity Component Systems (ECS) with SFML

Entity Component Systems (ECS) is a powerful architectural pattern used in game development to manage and organize game objects and their behaviors efficiently. By integrating ECS with SFML, you can build flexible and scalable game engines. In this section, we'll explore how to implement an ECS architecture alongside SFML for your game development projects.

Understanding Entity Component Systems (ECS)

ECS is a design pattern that separates the concerns of game objects into three main components:

1. **Entities**: These are placeholders for game objects and do not contain any behavior or data themselves.

2. **Components**: Components hold specific data and represent a single aspect or property of a game object, such as position, sprite, or health.

3. **Systems**: Systems contain the logic that operates on entities and their components. Each system focuses on a specific aspect of the game, such as rendering, physics, or input handling.

The key advantage of ECS is its flexibility. It allows you to create complex game objects by combining different components, and systems can operate on entities based on the components they possess.

Implementing ECS with SFML

To implement ECS with SFML, follow these steps:

1. **Define Your Components**: Identify the data that represents the properties of your game objects. Common components include Transform (position, rotation, scale), Sprite (for rendering), Physics (for collision detection), and Input (for user input).

2. **Create Your Entity-Component System**: Implement the core ECS framework, including the management of entities, components, and systems. You can use existing ECS libraries like EntityX or build your custom system.

3. **Initialize SFML**: Set up your SFML environment, including creating a window, loading resources (textures, sounds, etc.), and initializing the SFML main loop.

4. **Create Entities and Attach Components**: In your game, create entities and attach relevant components to them based on the object's properties. For example, a player character entity may have a Transform, Sprite, Input, and Physics component.

5. **Implement Systems**: Develop systems that operate on entities with specific sets of components. For instance, you may have a RenderingSystem that renders all entities with Sprite components, and a PhysicsSystem that handles collision detection and movement based on Physics components.

6. **Update and Render Loop**: In your SFML game loop, update the ECS systems in the correct order. This ensures that systems operate on entities in a controlled sequence. Additionally, render entities with the RenderingSystem to display them on the screen.

Here's a simplified example of an ECS-based game loop using SFML:

```cpp
// Initialize SFML
sf::RenderWindow window(sf::VideoMode(800, 600), "ECS with SFML");

// Create an ECS instance
ECS ecs;
```

```
// Game Loop
while (window.isOpen()) {
    sf::Event event;
    while (window.pollEvent(event)) {
        if (event.type == sf::Event::Closed) {
            window.close();
        }
    }

    // Update ECS systems
    ecs.update();

    // Clear the window
    window.clear();

    // Render entities with the RenderingSystem
    ecs.render(window);

    // Display the rendered frame
    window.display();
}
```

This example demonstrates the integration of ECS with SFML, providing a foundation for building complex and modular game systems. You can expand upon this architecture by adding more components and systems to suit your game's requirements.

Benefits of ECS with SFML

Integrating ECS with SFML offers several advantages:

1. **Modularity**: ECS promotes a modular approach to game development, making it easier to add, modify, or remove features.

2. **Performance**: ECS allows for efficient memory management and data locality, improving performance in resource-intensive games.

3. **Scalability**: You can scale your game engine to handle a large number of entities and systems without sacrificing performance.

4. **Code Reusability**: Components and systems can be reused across different projects, saving development time.

5. **Debugging**: ECS simplifies debugging by isolating systems and their interactions, making it easier to identify and fix issues.

By adopting ECS with SFML, you can create games that are not only more efficient but also more maintainable and extensible as your projects grow in complexity.

Section 10.4: Building a Custom Game Engine with Frameworks

Building a custom game engine from scratch is a significant undertaking that requires a deep understanding of game development, computer graphics, and low-level programming. However, with the help of existing frameworks and libraries like SFML, SDL, or Unity, you can streamline the process and focus on developing the unique features and gameplay of your game. In this section, we'll explore the process of building a custom game engine using such frameworks as a starting point.

Choosing the Right Framework

Before embarking on building your custom game engine, it's crucial to select the right framework or library that aligns with your project's goals. Here are some considerations:

1. **SFML**: If you're comfortable with C++ and want to create 2D games with a strong focus on multimedia capabilities (graphics, audio, and input), SFML is an excellent choice. It provides a solid foundation for building custom engines.

2. **SDL (Simple DirectMedia Layer)**: SDL is a C library that offers low-level access to audio, keyboard, mouse, joystick, and graphics hardware via OpenGL and Direct3D. It's suitable for building custom engines with more control over hardware interactions.

3. **Unity**: If you prefer a visual, cross-platform game engine with a strong community and asset store support, Unity might be the right choice. You can build custom gameplay systems and extend Unity's functionality using C# scripts.

4. **Unreal Engine**: Unreal Engine is a powerful game engine suitable for creating high-quality 3D games. While it's less focused on building custom engines, it offers extensive customization through UnrealScript or C++.

Building the Engine Foundation

Once you've chosen the framework that suits your needs, you can start building your custom game engine. Here's a high-level overview of the process:

1. **Setting Up the Project**: Create a new project using your chosen framework. Set up the necessary development environment, including compilers, IDEs, and build tools.

2. **Defining the Architecture**: Plan the architecture of your custom engine. Decide how you'll structure game objects, handle game logic, manage resources, and implement systems for rendering, physics, input, and audio.

3. **Creating a Game Loop**: Implement a game loop that updates the game's state, processes user input, and renders frames. Ensure that the loop runs at a consistent frame rate to provide a smooth gaming experience.

4. **Graphics and Rendering**: Depending on your chosen framework, integrate the rendering system. Configure shaders, materials, and rendering pipelines for 2D or 3D graphics. Implement efficient rendering techniques for optimal performance.

5. **Physics Simulation**: Integrate a physics engine or implement basic collision detection and response systems. Physics engines like Box2D or Bullet can be incorporated into your custom engine.

6. **Input Handling**: Develop a robust input system that handles keyboard, mouse, gamepad, and touch input. Map user input to in-game actions and events.

7. **Audio Management**: Implement audio playback and management systems. Load and play sound effects and music tracks. Consider 3D audio spatialization for immersive experiences.

8. **Resource Management**: Create a resource management system to load and manage game assets efficiently. This includes textures, models, sounds, and other content.

9. **Scripting and Game Logic**: Decide on a scripting language or system for implementing game logic. You can use Lua, JavaScript, or custom scripting languages, depending on your engine's design.

10. **Tools and Editors**: Develop tools and editors to streamline content creation, level design, and debugging. These tools can significantly improve your workflow.

11. **Testing and Debugging**: Thoroughly test your engine, identify bugs, and implement debugging tools. Ensure stability and performance across different hardware configurations.

12. **Documentation**: Document your engine's architecture, APIs, and usage. Clear documentation is essential for yourself and potential collaborators.

Leveraging Framework Features

While building a custom engine, remember that you can leverage the features and components provided by your chosen framework. For example, if you're using SFML, you can benefit from its rendering, audio, and input handling capabilities, allowing you to focus on higher-level gameplay systems.

Additionally, consider the community and available resources for your framework. Many frameworks have active communities, forums, and tutorials that can help you overcome challenges and learn best practices.

Building a custom game engine is a complex but rewarding endeavor. It offers full control over your game's technology stack and allows you to create unique gaming experiences. However, it's essential to balance customization with practicality, especially for smaller projects, as building an engine from scratch can be time-consuming.

Section 10.5: Exploring Advanced Features in Game Development Frameworks

Game development frameworks provide a solid foundation for creating games efficiently, but they often come with a wealth of advanced features that can take your games to the next level. In this section, we'll explore some of these advanced features that are commonly available in popular game development frameworks like Unity, Unreal Engine, and others.

1. Advanced Graphics and Rendering Techniques

Most game development frameworks support advanced graphics rendering techniques that can make your games visually stunning. These include:

- **Real-time Lighting**: Implement dynamic lighting and shadows to create realistic and immersive scenes. Unity's Universal Render Pipeline and Unreal Engine's lighting system are excellent examples.

- **Particle Systems**: Simulate complex particle effects like fire, smoke, water splashes, and magical spells. These systems can enhance the visual appeal of your games.

- **Post-Processing Effects**: Apply post-processing effects like bloom, motion blur, depth of field, and color grading to achieve a cinematic look.

- **GPU Programming**: Utilize the power of the GPU to implement custom shaders and graphics effects. Shader languages like HLSL (High-Level Shading Language) and GLSL (OpenGL Shading Language) are commonly used.

2. Physics Simulation

Game frameworks often come with robust physics engines that enable realistic interactions between objects. You can leverage features like:

- **Ragdoll Physics**: Create characters and creatures with realistic physics-based animations, allowing them to react dynamically to external forces.

- **Soft Body Physics**: Simulate deformable objects like cloth, rubber, or jelly with soft body physics, adding a tactile feel to your game.

- **Vehicle Physics**: Implement realistic vehicle physics for cars, planes, and other vehicles, enhancing the driving and flying experiences.

3. Advanced AI and Pathfinding

Frameworks provide tools for advanced AI behaviors and pathfinding:

- **Behavior Trees**: Create complex AI behaviors using behavior trees, a visual scripting approach that allows you to design intricate decision-making processes.

- **Machine Learning Integration**: Some frameworks support integrating machine learning models to create adaptive AI that learns from player behavior.

- **Navigation Meshes**: Implement navigation meshes for efficient pathfinding in complex environments, ensuring NPCs and characters move intelligently.

4. Multiplayer and Networking

To build online multiplayer games, frameworks offer features such as:

- **Multiplayer APIs**: Access networking APIs to handle client-server communication, synchronization, and real-time gameplay for multiplayer experiences.

- **Dedicated Servers**: Implement dedicated game servers to host multiplayer matches, allowing players to connect and play together.

- **Lobby and Matchmaking Systems**: Create matchmaking systems that pair players of similar skill levels and provide lobbies for player interaction.

5. Animation and Cinematics

Frameworks support advanced animation and cinematic tools for storytelling:

- **Cutscene Editors**: Use visual editors to create cinematic sequences, including camera animations, character animations, and scripted events.

- **Timeline Systems**: Implement timeline systems that allow you to sequence events and animations precisely, controlling the pacing of your game.

- **Cinematic Cameras**: Use cinematic camera tools to create dynamic and engaging camera angles for storytelling.

6. Augmented Reality (AR) and Virtual Reality (VR)

For AR and VR experiences, some frameworks provide specialized features:

- **AR Integration**: Access AR features like marker detection, image recognition, and real-world object tracking for augmented reality applications.

- **VR Support**: Create VR experiences by leveraging VR headset integration, hand tracking, and motion controllers.

7. Audio and Sound Design

Frameworks offer tools for immersive audio experiences:

- **Spatial Audio**: Implement 3D audio spatialization to create realistic soundscapes where audio sources change based on the player's position and orientation.

- **Interactive Music**: Create interactive music systems that adapt to gameplay situations, intensifying or relaxing based on in-game events.

8. Scripting and Extensibility

Many frameworks support scripting languages like C#, Python, or Lua, allowing you to extend and customize the engine's functionality. You can create custom gameplay mechanics, tools, and editor extensions to streamline your development process.

9. Analytics and Telemetry

Frameworks often include analytics and telemetry tools to gather player data and insights. You can track player behavior, monitor game performance, and make data-driven decisions for game improvements.

10. Cross-Platform Development

Game development frameworks excel at cross-platform development, allowing you to deploy your games on multiple platforms with minimal effort. Ensure your game reaches a wide audience by targeting various platforms, including PC, consoles, mobile devices, and the web.

Incorporating these advanced features into your game development project can significantly enhance gameplay, visual quality, and player engagement. However, it's essential to balance the use of these features with the scope and goals of your game, ensuring they contribute to a cohesive and enjoyable player experience.

Chapter 11: Implementing Multi-Chapter Projects

Section 11.1: The Benefits of Multi-Chapter Projects

In the world of software development, projects can vary widely in scope and complexity. While many projects are relatively small and self-contained, there are cases where it becomes necessary to tackle larger and more ambitious endeavors. Multi-chapter projects are a prime example of this. These projects consist of multiple interconnected chapters, often forming a cohesive whole, such as a video game with different levels or episodes.

Understanding the Structure

A multi-chapter project typically consists of several individual chapters or segments, each with its unique content, objectives, and challenges. These chapters can be thought of as building blocks, and they are designed to fit together seamlessly to create a unified user experience. In the context of game development, each chapter might represent a level or a distinct part of the game world.

Benefits of Multi-Chapter Projects

1. *Progressive Complexity:* *One significant advantage of multi-chapter projects is the ability to gradually increase complexity. The early chapters can serve as an introduction to the core mechanics, allowing users to build their skills and understanding before facing more challenging content. This progressive learning curve is common in video games and educational software.*

2. *Narrative and Storytelling:* *For projects with a narrative component, such as video games or interactive stories, multi-chapter structures allow for the development of intricate and engaging plots. Each chapter can contribute to the overall narrative, introducing new characters, plot twists, and conflicts.*

3. *Variety and Exploration:* *Different chapters can offer a diverse range of environments, gameplay mechanics, and challenges. This variety keeps users engaged and provides opportunities for exploration and experimentation.*

4. *Modular Development:* *From a development perspective, multi-chapter projects promote modular development practices. Each chapter can be developed independently, allowing teams to work on different parts of the project simultaneously. This modularity simplifies testing and debugging and can lead to more efficient development.*

5. *Longevity and Replayability:* *Multi-chapter projects can have a longer shelf life and higher replayability. Users may return to earlier chapters to explore alternative paths or achieve higher scores, increasing the project's overall longevity.*

Challenges to Consider

While multi-chapter projects offer numerous benefits, they also come with challenges, including:

- **Consistency:** Maintaining consistency in terms of art, design, and mechanics across chapters can be challenging.
- **Testing:** Comprehensive testing and quality assurance are crucial to ensure that all chapters work seamlessly together.
- **Resource Management:** Managing assets, such as art, music, and code, across chapters requires careful planning.
- **User Engagement:** Keeping users engaged throughout the entire project can be a design and development challenge.

In summary, multi-chapter projects offer an effective way to create rich, engaging, and modular software experiences. They provide a structured approach to progressive complexity, storytelling, and variety while presenting development teams with both opportunities and challenges.

Section 11.2: Designing a Multi-Chapter Game

Designing a multi-chapter game is a complex process that requires careful planning and consideration of various factors. Whether you're creating a video game with multiple levels, an episodic adventure, or an educational software package, here are key steps and principles to follow:

1. Define the Core Concept:

Start by defining the core concept or theme of your multi-chapter game. What is the central idea or story that will tie all the chapters together? This concept should guide the development of each chapter's content and gameplay.

2. Create a Storyline or Progression:

If your game has a narrative element, outline the storyline or progression that will unfold across the chapters. Consider how each chapter contributes to the overall narrative arc. Plan key plot points, character introductions, and conflicts.

3. Chapter Objectives and Themes:

Each chapter should have its own objectives and themes that align with the core concept. Determine what players should achieve or experience in each chapter. This could include acquiring new skills, facing unique challenges, or exploring different environments.

4. Consistent Art and Design:

Maintain consistency in art style, design elements, and user interface across all chapters. A cohesive visual identity helps create a unified and immersive user experience. Create design guidelines to ensure consistency.

5. Gameplay Progression:

Plan the progression of gameplay mechanics and difficulty. Early chapters should introduce fundamental mechanics and gradually increase complexity. Later chapters can challenge players with more advanced gameplay elements.

6. Recurring Elements:

Consider incorporating recurring elements or motifs that tie chapters together. This could be a recurring character, item, or gameplay mechanic that players encounter throughout the game.

7. Testing and Balancing:

Thoroughly playtest each chapter to identify and address bugs, balance issues, and gameplay improvements. Pay attention to user feedback to refine the overall experience.

8. Chapter Interconnections:

If your multi-chapter game allows players to revisit previous chapters or make choices that affect later ones, ensure these interconnections are well-implemented. Choices made in one chapter should have meaningful consequences in others.

9. Chapter Navigation and Progression:

Design clear and intuitive navigation between chapters. Provide players with a sense of progress and a way to track their completion of each chapter.

10. User Engagement and Retention:
Consider strategies to keep players engaged throughout the entire experience. This may involve including achievements, collectibles, or incentives for replaying chapters.

11. Documentation and Resources:
Create documentation for your development team that outlines the design, objectives, and technical requirements of each chapter. Ensure easy access to shared resources, such as art assets and code libraries.

12. Scalability and Future Expansion:
Plan for scalability and the potential addition of new chapters or content in the future. Design your architecture to accommodate expansions without major rework.

13. User Feedback and Iteration:
After releasing your multi-chapter game, actively seek user feedback and iterate on the experience. Use analytics to understand player behavior and make data-driven improvements.

14. Cross-Platform Considerations:

If your game targets multiple platforms, address cross-platform challenges ea rly in development. Ensure consistent performance and user experience across different devices and operating systems.

Designing a multi-chapter game is a creative and logistical endeavor that requires a balance between storytelling, gameplay, and technical execution. With careful planning and attention to detail, you can create a compelling and immersive experience that captivates players across multiple chapters.

Section 11.3: Managing Assets and Resources Across Chapters

In a multi-chapter game, efficient management of assets and resources is crucial to ensure a smooth and cohesive player experience. Here, we'll explore strategies for handling assets, resources, and data across chapters.

1. Asset Organization:

Start by organizing your assets logically. Create a clear folder structure to categorize assets such as images, audio files, 3D models, and scripts. Use meaningful names and subdirectories to make asset retrieval straightforward.

2. Asset Loading and Unloading:

Load and unload assets dynamically as needed. In each chapter, determine which assets are required and load them at the appropriate time. When transitioning between chapters, unload assets that are no longer necessary to free up memory.

3. Resource Pools:

Implement resource pools for frequently used assets like character models or sound effects. These pools can be initialized at the beginning of the game and reused across chapters to reduce loading times.

4. Asset References:

Use asset references rather than hardcoding file paths. This allows you to change asset locations or filenames without altering code. Libraries like Asset Bundles (Unity) or Asset Management Systems (Unreal Engine) can help manage references efficiently.

5. Data Serialization:

Serialize game data such as player progress, achievements, and unlocked content. Use a format like JSON or XML to save and load this data between chapters. This ensures continuity when players revisit previous chapters.

6. Streaming Assets:

For larger assets or open-world environments, consider implementing streaming techniques. Load only the portions of the map or assets that are currently visible to the player to optimize performance.

7. Cross-Chapter Resources:

Identify assets and resources that need to persist across chapters. These might include player inventory, character stats, or global settings. Implement a mechanism to carry this data from one chapter to the next.

8. Resource Versioning:

Maintain version control for assets and resources. When updating or adding new content, ensure compatibility with existing chapters. Consider using version numbers or metadata to track changes.

9. Resource Compression:

Compress assets to reduce storage requirements and improve loading times. Choose appropriate compression formats for images, audio, and 3D models. Balance compression with quality to maintain visual and auditory fidelity.

10. Loading Screens:

Implement loading screens or transitions between chapters to manage player expectations. These screens can provide hints or lore related to the upcoming chapter and create a smoother experience.

11. Localization and Internationalization:

If your game supports multiple languages, plan for localization across all chapters. Keep text and audio files separate for easy translation and adaptation.

12. Asset Bundling:

Consider bundling assets specific to each chapter. This can help reduce the size of initial downloads or installations for players and streamline content updates.

13. Cross-Platform Compatibility:

Ensure that asset formats and resource management are compatible across all target platforms. Different platforms may have specific requirements or limitations.

14. Testing and Optimization:

Regularly test your asset management system to identify bottlenecks or memory leaks. Optimize asset loading and unloading routines to minimize hiccups in gameplay.

15. Error Handling:

```
Implement robust error handling for asset loading failures. Provide informati
ve error messages or fallback assets to prevent crashes or missing content.
```

Efficient asset and resource management is a cornerstone of successful multi-chapter game development. It not only ensures a seamless player experience but also simplifies content updates and future expansion. By following these best practices, you can create a cohesive and engaging gaming experience that spans multiple chapters.

Section 11.4: Synchronizing Game State Across Chapters

Maintaining consistent game state across chapters is a critical aspect of multi-chapter game development. Players expect their progress, choices, and achievements to carry over seamlessly as they progress through the story. Here, we'll explore strategies for synchronizing game state effectively.

1. Save and Load Mechanism:

Implement a robust save and load system that allows players to save their progress at any point and load it when starting a new chapter. Save files should store essential game state data, such as character stats, inventory, and completed quests.

2. Cross-Chapter Events:

Use event-driven programming to trigger actions or updates when transitioning between chapters. Define events and listeners to handle actions like awarding achievements, changing character relationships, or adjusting global variables.

3. Player Choices and Consequences:

Ensure that player choices made in previous chapters influence the narrative and gameplay in subsequent ones. Develop a system that records and interprets these choices, affecting dialogues, character reactions, and available quests.

4. Persistent Variables:

Identify variables and data that should persist across chapters, such as the player's name, accumulated experience points, or reputation with in-game factions. Store these as global variables or in a centralized data repository.

5. Achievements and Rewards:

Design an achievement system that tracks player accomplishments throughout the game. Recognize and reward achievements with in-game items, skills, or narrative consequences. Players should see their achievements reflected in later chapters.

6. Narrative Continuity:

Maintain narrative continuity by referencing past events and decisions. Include callbacks to prior chapters in dialogues and storylines to provide a sense of coherence and immersion.

7. Dynamic Content Generation:

Generate dynamic content based on player progress. For instance, unlock new areas, quests, or characters as the player advances. Adapt the game's content to the player's choices and achievements.

8. Testing and QA:

Thoroughly test game state synchronization by playing through different chapter combinations. Pay attention to edge cases, unexpected player choices, and the impact of updates and patches on saved games.

9. Version Compatibility:

Ensure backward compatibility of save files when releasing updates or patches. Players should be able to continue their existing games without issues after a game update.

10. Optimized Data Handling:

Optimize data structures and algorithms for handling game state. Large datasets should load efficiently, and you should avoid unnecessary data duplication.

11. Error Handling:

Implement error handling and recovery mechanisms for scenarios where data corruption or unexpected changes occur in saved games. Provide clear error messages and options for recovery.

12. Cloud Saves and Cross-Platform Play:

If your game supports multiple platforms, consider implementing cloud save functionality. This allows players to access their save files from different devices and ensures consistency.

13. User Feedback:

Encourage players to provide feedback on game state synchronization issues. Use player feedback to identify and resolve problems and improve the overall player experience.

14. Post-Launch Support:

Commit to providing post-launch support for synchronization issues. Addressing player concerns and maintaining consistent game state can lead to positive player reviews and long-term engagement.

15. Documentation:

Document your game's synchronization mechanisms, especially if you plan to involve other developers or teams. Clear documentation ensures that everyone understands how game state is managed.

Synchronizing game state across chapters is a complex but rewarding endeavor. It enhances player immersion and engagement by making their choices and progress matter throughout the entire game. By implementing these strategies and paying attention to detail, you can create a compelling and coherent multi-chapter gaming experience.

Section 11.5: Cross-Platform Deployment for Multi-Chapter Projects

Cross-platform deployment is a crucial aspect of multi-chapter game development, as it ensures that your game can reach a wide audience across various platforms and devices. In this section, we'll explore strategies and considerations for deploying multi-chapter projects to different platforms.

1. Platform Selection:

Before starting deployment, decide which platforms you want to target. Common platforms include Windows, macOS, Linux, iOS, Android, and game consoles. Each platform may have specific requirements and limitations, so research them thoroughly.

2. Development Environments:

Set up the development environments for each target platform. This may involve using different IDEs (Integrated Development Environments), compilers, and SDKs (Software Development Kits). Familiarize yourself with platform-specific tools and documentation.

3. Code Portability:

Write your game code with portability in mind. Use cross-platform libraries and frameworks like SFML to abstract platform-specific functionality. Minimize platform-specific code by encapsulating it in separate modules or classes.

4. Testing and Debugging:

Regularly test your game on each target platform to identify and address platform-specific issues. Debugging tools and techniques may vary, so be prepared to adapt your debugging process accordingly.

5. User Interface Adaptation:

Tailor your game's user interface (UI) to fit the requirements of each platform. Consider differences in screen sizes, resolutions, and input methods. Implement responsive design to ensure a consistent and enjoyable user experience.

6. Performance Optimization:

Optimize your game's performance for each platform. This may involve adjusting graphics settings, resource loading, and memory management to ensure smooth gameplay on lower-end devices.

7. Compliance and Certification:

Platforms like app stores and consoles often require certification before you can publish your game. Familiarize yourself with their submission guidelines, content restrictions, and certification processes. Ensure your game complies with age ratings and legal requirements.

8. Localization:

If you plan to release your game in different regions, consider localization. Translate in-game text, audio, and subtitles to cater to a global audience. Adapt cultural references and symbols to be inclusive and respectful.

9. Version Control and Build Management:

Use version control systems like Git to manage your project's source code. Maintain separate branches for each platform to facilitate platform-specific development. Implement a robust build management system to automate the creation of platform-specific builds.

10. Cross-Platform Testing:

Create a comprehensive testing plan that covers all target platforms. Test gameplay, UI, performance, and functionality thoroughly on each platform. Pay special attention to platform-specific features and interactions.

11. Distribution Channels:

Decide how you will distribute your game on each platform. Options include app stores, online marketplaces, direct downloads from your website, and physical copies for consoles. Ensure your distribution channels align with platform requirements.

12. Post-Launch Support:

After launching your game, continue to provide post-launch support. Address platform-specific issues, release updates, and stay informed about changes in platform policies and technologies.

13. Community Engagement:

Build and engage with a community of players on each platform. Listen to feedback, respond to player inquiries, and participate in platform-specific forums and social media channels.

14. Analytics and Metrics:

Use analytics tools to gather data on player behavior, engagement, and performance across platforms. Analyze this data to make informed decisions about updates and improvements.

15. Legal Considerations:

Be aware of legal considerations when deploying your game. This includes intellectual property rights, licensing agreements, and compliance with privacy and data protection regulations.

16. Cross-Platform Promotion:
Promote your game effectively on each platform. Customize marketing materials , screenshots, and trailers for different audiences. Leverage platform-specific advertising options and partnerships.

17. Feedback and Iteration:
Encourage players to provide feedback and iterate on your game based on their suggestions. Implementing player-driven improvements can enhance the overall player experience on all platforms.

18. Accessibility:
Ensure your game is accessible to players with disabilities. Implement features like customizable controls, text-to-speech, and colorblind-friendly options to make your game inclusive.

Cross-platform deployment for multi-chapter projects requires careful planning, development, and testing. By following these strategies and considerations, you can reach a broad audience while providing a consistent and enjoyable gaming experience across various platforms and devices.

Chapter 12: Cross-Platform Coding and Best Practices

Section 12.1: Writing Cross-Platform Code Efficiently

Writing cross-platform code efficiently is a fundamental skill for developers working on projects that need to run on multiple operating systems or platforms. Whether you're targeting desktop, mobile, or embedded systems, adopting best practices for cross-platform coding can save time, reduce maintenance efforts, and ensure a consistent user experience across different environments.

1. Use Cross-Platform Libraries and Frameworks:

Leverage cross-platform libraries and frameworks like SFML, Qt, or SDL. These libraries provide a common abstraction layer for platform-specific functionality, allowing you to write code that works across multiple systems.

2. Conditional Compilation:

Use preprocessor directives or conditional compilation flags to isolate platform-specific code. For example, you can use #ifdef and #ifndef macros to include or exclude sections of code based on the target platform.

```
#ifdef _WIN32
// Windows-specific code
#elif __linux__
// Linux-specific code
#elif __APPLE__
// macOS-specific code
#endif
```

3. Abstract Platform Differences:

Create wrapper classes or functions to abstract platform differences. This approach allows you to encapsulate platform-specific code in a way that's transparent to the rest of your application.

```
// Example of abstracting file system operations
class PlatformFileSystem {
public:
    static bool FileExists(const std::string& filePath);
    // ... other platform-specific functions
};
```

4. Avoid Non-Standard Features:

Refrain from using platform-specific or non-standard C/C++ features. Stick to the C++ standard library and language features to ensure code portability. Be cautious with compiler extensions and language features that are not part of the standard.

5. Modularize Your Code:

Divide your codebase into well-defined modules with clear interfaces. This modular approach allows you to replace or extend specific modules for different platforms while keeping the core logic intact.

6. Test Early and Often:

Regularly test your code on all target platforms during development. Use continuous integration (CI) pipelines to automate testing on different environments. This helps catch platform-specific issues early.

7. Version Control and Branching:

Use version control systems (e.g., Git) and branching strategies to manage platform-specific code. Create branches for platform-specific development and merge changes back into the main codebase when they are stable.

8. Documentation:

Document platform-specific code, dependencies, and build instructions comprehensively. This documentation is invaluable when onboarding new team members or revisiting the codebase after some time.

9. Stay Informed:

Keep up-to-date with platform-specific updates, changes, and best practices. Platforms, compilers, and libraries evolve, and staying informed helps you adapt your codebase accordingly.

10. Error Handling and Logging:

Implement robust error handling and logging mechanisms. Make sure error messages and logs are informative and platform-agnostic, aiding debugging and troubleshooting.

11. Cross-Platform Tools:

Utilize cross-platform development tools and build systems such as CMake or P remake. These tools help manage project configurations and generate platform-specific build files.

12. Build Automation:

Automate the build process to create consistent builds across different platforms. Use build scripts or build automation tools like Jenkins or Travis CI to streamline this process.

13. Cross-Platform Compatibility Testing:

Conduct comprehensive compatibility testing on target platforms. Verify that the application functions as expected and meets performance requirements on all supported environments.

14. Performance Optimization:

Optimize your code for performance on each platform. Consider platform-specific optimizations when necessary, but maintain a balance to ensure code remains portable.

15. Security Considerations:

Be aware of security differences between platforms. Implement security best practices and consider platform-specific security features or configurations.

16. Feedback and Collaboration:

Foster collaboration among team members with expertise in different platforms. Encourage open communication and knowledge sharing to tackle platform-specific challenges effectively.

Efficiently writing cross-platform code requires a combination of skills, tools, and best practices. By following these guidelines, you can develop software that runs seamlessly on various platforms while minimizing the complexities of platform-specific development.

Section 12.2: Handling Differences in Compiler and Library Versions

Handling differences in compiler and library versions is a crucial aspect of cross-platform coding. Software projects often depend on specific compiler features and library versions, and when you target multiple platforms, you encounter variations in toolchains and libraries. Managing these differences effectively ensures that your code compiles and runs reliably across various environments.

1. Use Compiler Directives:

Compiler-specific directives, also known as pragmas or attributes, can help manage compiler-specific code. For instance, you can use #pragma directives to set compiler options or disable specific warnings on a per-compiler basis.

```
#ifdef _MSC_VER
#pragma warning(disable: 4996) // Disable a specific warning on MSVC
#endif
```

2. Compiler Feature Checks:

To handle differences in compiler features, use preprocessor macros to check for feature support. This allows you to conditionally include or exclude code based on compiler capabilities.

```
#ifdef __cplusplus
#if __cplusplus >= 201703L
// Code for C++17 and above
#endif
#endif
```

3. Library Version Checks:

When dealing with external libraries, check for specific library versions to ensure compatibility. Many libraries provide version macros that you can use to enable or disable features based on library versions.

```
#include <library.h>

#if LIBRARY_VERSION >= 200
// Code compatible with library version 2.0.0 and above
#endif
```

4. Conditional Compilation Blocks:

Organize code in conditional compilation blocks to handle variations in library APIs or features. These blocks make it easier to manage code that differs between library versions.

```
#ifdef LIBRARY_VERSION_2_0
// Code specific to version 2.0
#else
// Code for other library versions
#endif
```

5. Custom Configuration Files:

Create custom configuration files that define platform-specific settings and dependencies. These files can be included selectively based on the target platform, simplifying the management of compiler and library differences.

```
#ifdef PLATFORM_WINDOWS
#include "config_windows.h"
#endif
```

6. Compiler Abstraction Layers:

Develop compiler abstraction layers if your project targets multiple compilers. These layers encapsulate compiler-specific code and provide a uniform interface for your application.

```
// CompilerAbstraction.h
#pragma once

#ifdef _MSC_VER
#include "CompilerAbstraction_MSVC.h"
#endif

// ...
```

7. Documentation and Comments:

Document compiler and library requirements, including minimum versions and specific features. Include comments in your code that explain why certain code sections exist, especially when they are compiler or library-dependent.

8. Continuous Integration Testing:

Implement continuous integration (CI) testing on different platforms and compiler versions. CI systems can automatically build and test your code on various configurations, helping catch compatibility issues early.

9. Community and Forum Support:

If you encounter platform-specific challenges, seek help from developer communities and forums dedicated to the platforms or libraries you are using. Experienced developers can often provide guidance on handling version-specific issues.

10. Fallback Mechanisms:
Consider implementing fallback mechanisms for features that may not be availa ble in older library or compiler versions. These fallbacks allow your code to gracefully handle unsupported features.

11. Stay Updated:
Keep track of updates to compilers and libraries. New versions may introduce features that simplify cross-platform development or resolve compatibility is sues.

12. Version Management Tools:
Use version management tools like CMake or Conan to specify required compiler and library versions in your project's build configuration. These tools can h elp automate dependency management.

Handling differences in compiler and library versions requires vigilance and careful planning. By employing these strategies, you can minimize the challenges associated with variations in toolchains and libraries, ensuring that your cross-platform projects compile and run smoothly across different environments.

Section 12.3: Debugging and Profiling on Multiple Platforms

Debugging and profiling are essential aspects of software development. When working on cross-platform projects, it's crucial to have a solid strategy for debugging and profiling code across different platforms and environments. In this section, we'll explore various techniques and tools to facilitate debugging and profiling in cross-platform development.

1. Platform-Specific Debugging Tools:

Different platforms offer their debugging tools. Familiarize yourself with platform-specific debuggers, such as GDB for Linux, LLDB for macOS, and WinDbg for Windows. These tools allow you to inspect and debug your code at a low level.

2. Cross-Platform Debugging with IDEs:

Integrated Development Environments (IDEs) like Visual Studio, CLion, and Code::Blocks provide cross-platform debugging capabilities. They allow you to debug code on various platforms within a single development environment.

3. Remote Debugging:

For cross-platform projects, you can perform remote debugging. This involves running the application on one platform while debugging it from another. Tools like GDB and LLDB support remote debugging, enabling you to debug code running on a different machine or platform.

4. Conditional Logging:

Implement conditional logging to output debug information. Use preprocessor directives to enable or disable logging based on compilation flags. This helps minimize the overhead of debugging code in release builds.

```
#ifdef DEBUG_MODE
// Debug-specific logging
#endif
```

5. Assertions:

Use assertions to check the correctness of code assumptions. Assertions are especially useful during development and debugging phases, as they can help identify issues early.

```
assert(expression); // Halts execution if 'expression' is false
```

6. Profiling Tools:

Profiling tools like Valgrind, Instruments (for macOS), and VTune (for Intel processors) help identify performance bottlenecks in your code. These tools provide insights into memory usage, CPU usage, and function call traces.

7. Cross-Platform Profiling:

Some profiling tools offer cross-platform support. For example, tools like Google's CPU Profiler can be used on multiple platforms to analyze code performance.

8. Performance Counters:

Many platforms provide performance counters that allow you to gather data on various hardware metrics, such as CPU cycles, cache misses, and memory bandwidth. These counters can be accessed and analyzed programmatically to fine-tune code performance.

9. Benchmarking:

Implement benchmarking tests to measure the execution time of specific code sections. Tools like Google Benchmark can help you compare the performance of code across different platforms.

10. Log Analysis:

Collect and analyze logs generated by your application on various platforms. Log aggregation tools like ELK Stack (Elasticsearch, Logstash, and Kibana) can help centralize and analyze logs from multiple sources.

11. Error Reporting Mechanisms:

Implement mechanisms for collecting and reporting errors from deployed applications. Error reports can provide valuable information for debugging issues in the field.

12. Continuous Integration Testing:

Integrate debugging and profiling into your continuous integration (CI) pipeline. Automated tests and profiling runs on various platforms can help catch issues early and ensure consistent performance.

13. Platform-Specific Quirks:

Be aware of platform-specific quirks that can affect debugging and profiling. Different platforms may have different behaviors or limitations when it comes to debugging and profiling tools.

14. Documentation and Knowledge Sharing:

Document debugging and profiling procedures specific to each platform in your project's documentation. Share knowledge and best practices among your development team to ensure efficient debugging and profiling workflows.

Debugging and profiling in cross-platform development can be challenging due to the diversity of environments and tools involved. However, by leveraging platform-specific and cross-platform debugging and profiling tools, implementing conditional logging, and following best practices, you can effectively identify and address issues in your code, ensuring that your software performs optimally on various platforms.

Section 12.4: Managing Cross-Platform Dependencies

Cross-platform development often involves dealing with external libraries, frameworks, and dependencies. Managing these dependencies efficiently is crucial to ensure that your project can be built and run smoothly on multiple platforms. In this section, we'll explore strategies for managing cross-platform dependencies in your development workflow.

1. Package Managers:

Consider using package managers like CMake, vcpkg, Conan, or Hunter to handle dependencies. These tools can help automate the process of downloading, configuring, and building external libraries for different platforms.

2. Dependency Files:

Maintain a clear list of dependencies and their versions in a dedicated file (e.g., CMakeLists.txt, conanfile.txt, or package.json). This makes it easier to manage and share dependency information across your development team.

```
find_package(SFML 2.5 REQUIRED)
```

3. Conditional Compilation:

Use preprocessor directives and conditional compilation to adapt your code to different platforms and dependencies. This allows you to include or exclude specific code sections based on the target platform or dependency availability.

```
#ifdef _WIN32
// Windows-specific code
#endif

#ifndef HAS_SFML
// Code for when SFML is not available
#endif
```

4. CMake and Find Modules:

If you're using CMake as your build system, create custom CMake "Find" modules for your dependencies. These modules can help CMake find and configure dependencies on various platforms automatically.

5. Dependency Isolation:

Consider using techniques like static linking or packaging dependencies alongside your application, especially for smaller libraries. This can simplify deployment by reducing external dependencies.

6. Cross-Compilation:

Cross-compile dependencies for your target platforms when feasible. This can save time and ensure that dependencies are built correctly for each platform.

7. Continuous Integration (CI):

Set up CI pipelines that automatically build and test your project on different platforms. This helps ensure that dependencies are correctly resolved and integrated into your cross-platform workflow.

8. Documentation:

Maintain clear documentation that outlines the steps required to set up and configure dependencies for each platform. Include platform-specific instructions and troubleshooting tips.

9. Dependency Licensing:

Be mindful of licensing issues when including third-party libraries in your project. Some licenses may have restrictions or require attribution, which can impact your cross-platform distribution.

10. Version Compatibility:
Regularly check for updates and new versions of dependencies. Ensure that the versions you're using are compatible with the target platforms and the rest o f your project.

11. Version Locking:
Depending on your project's stability and requirements, consider "locking" de pendency versions to avoid unexpected updates that might introduce breaking c hanges.

12. Testing on All Platforms:
Test your application on all target platforms to ensure that dependencies wor k as expected and that there are no platform-specific issues.

13. Fallback Mechanisms:
Implement fallback mechanisms or alternative code paths for situations where a specific dependency is unavailable on a particular platform. This ensures g raceful degradation of functionality.

Managing cross-platform dependencies can be complex, but with the right tools, documentation, and practices, you can streamline the process and ensure that your project runs smoothly on diverse platforms. Be proactive in handling dependencies, and regularly update and test your project to maintain compatibility and reliability across all target platforms.

Section 12.5: Best Practices for Cross-Platform Development

Cross-platform development can be challenging, but following best practices can make the process more manageable and help you avoid common pitfalls. In this section, we'll explore some essential best practices for successful cross-platform development.

1. Start with a Clear Plan:

Before diving into development, define your target platforms, system requirements, and any platform-specific features you need to support. Having a clear plan helps you make informed decisions throughout the development process.

2. Use Cross-Platform Libraries and Tools:

Whenever possible, choose cross-platform libraries, frameworks, and development tools. Libraries like SFML are designed to simplify cross-platform development by abstracting platform-specific details.

3. Separate Platform-Dependent Code:

Isolate platform-specific code into separate modules or files. Use conditional compilation (e.g., preprocessor directives in C++) to manage platform-specific code branches.

4. Testing on Real Hardware:

Test your application on real devices and platforms whenever possible. Emulators and simulators are useful for initial testing, but real hardware can uncover platform-specific issues that may not be apparent in simulations.

5. Continuous Integration (CI):

Implement a CI pipeline that automatically builds and tests your application on different platforms. CI helps catch issues early and ensures your code remains compatible with all target platforms.

6. Version Control and Collaboration:

Use version control systems like Git to manage your codebase. Collaborate with a team efficiently, and consider using branching strategies that support cross-platform development workflows.

7. Documentation:

Maintain comprehensive documentation for your project. Include platform-specific setup instructions, dependencies, and troubleshooting tips. Documentation helps both your development team and end-users.

8. Localization and Internationalization:

Plan for localization and internationalization from the start. Ensure that your application can support multiple languages and regions, including platform-specific considerations for input methods and date/time formats.

9. Performance Optimization:

Pay attention to performance optimization on each platform. What works efficiently on one platform may not be the best approach on another. Profiling tools can help identify platform-specific bottlenecks.

10. Security Considerations:
Be aware of platform-specific security considerations, such as permissions and access control. Follow best practices for secure coding and data handling to protect your application and its users.

11. Update and Maintenance Strategy:
Plan for post-release updates and maintenance. Be prepared to address platform-specific issues that may arise as new updates or patches for platforms are released.

12. User Feedback and Bug Reporting:
Establish clear channels for users to report platform-specific issues and provide feedback. Actively monitor user feedback and prioritize platform-related bug fixes.

13. User Experience (UX) Testing:
Conduct user experience testing on all target platforms. Ensure that the application provides a consistent and intuitive user experience across different devices and screen sizes.

14. Legal and Licensing Compliance:
Be aware of legal and licensing requirements for distributing your application on different platforms. Some platforms have specific guidelines and restrictions.

15. Stay Informed:
Stay up-to-date with platform-specific updates, guidelines, and best practices. Platforms can change over time, and staying informed ensures your application remains compatible.

Cross-platform development requires careful planning, attention to detail, and ongoing maintenance. By following these best practices, you can create high-quality applications that run smoothly on various platforms while minimizing the challenges and complexities of cross-platform development.

Chapter 13: Advanced Networking with SFML

Section 13.1: Networked Applications and Games

Networking is a fundamental aspect of modern software development, allowing applications and games to communicate and interact over the internet or local networks. In this section, we'll explore the importance of networking in software development and how SFML provides the tools needed to create networked applications and games.

Understanding Networked Applications

Networked applications, also known as networked software or distributed systems, are programs that run on multiple devices and communicate with each other to perform tasks collaboratively. These applications enable data sharing, remote control, real-time updates, and more. Examples of networked applications include online multiplayer games, chat applications, remote desktop software, and cloud-based services.

The Role of Networking in Games

In the context of game development, networking plays a critical role in enabling multiplayer and online gaming experiences. Multiplayer games allow players from around the world to connect, compete, and cooperate in real time. Networking is responsible for synchronizing game states, handling player interactions, and transmitting data between game clients and servers.

Here are some key aspects of networking in games:

1. **Client-Server Architecture:** Many multiplayer games use a client-server architecture. Clients are the game instances running on players' devices, while servers manage the game world and facilitate communication between clients.

2. **Latency and Lag:** Networked games must account for network latency, which can lead to lag or delays in gameplay. Optimizing network code is essential to minimize these effects.

3. **Security and Authentication:** Games must implement secure authentication and data transfer mechanisms to prevent cheating and protect user data.

4. **Data Serialization:** Game data, such as player positions, actions, and game events, must be serialized (converted into a format suitable for transmission) and deserialized on the receiving end.

5. **Scalability:** Online games must be designed to scale to support a large number of players simultaneously. Load balancing and server redundancy may be necessary.

SFML includes a networking module that provides a cross-platform API for handling network communication. This module allows developers to create both client and server applications, making it suitable for a wide range of networked software.

Some key features of SFML's networking module include:

- **TCP and UDP Protocols:** SFML supports both TCP (Transmission Control Protocol) and UDP (User Datagram Protocol), giving developers flexibility in choosing the appropriate protocol for their applications.

- **Socket Types:** SFML provides socket classes for TCP and UDP, making it easy to create network connections and send/receive data.

- **Packet Class:** The `sf::Packet` class simplifies data serialization and deserialization, streamlining network communication.

- **Networking Threads:** SFML's networking module can be used in conjunction with threading to handle network communication concurrently, ensuring smooth gameplay in networked games.

In the following sections, we'll dive deeper into using SFML's networking module to implement networked gameplay and explore various aspects of networked application development.

Section 13.2: Implementing Networked Gameplay with SFML

Implementing networked gameplay in games is an exciting but complex endeavor. In this section, we will explore how to use SFML's networking module to create networked games, focusing on the practical aspects of setting up client-server communication and synchronizing game states.

Client-Server Architecture

Most networked games use a client-server architecture, where one player acts as the server, and others (clients) connect to it. The server is responsible for maintaining the authoritative game state, validating player actions, and broadcasting updates to clients.

Here's a high-level overview of how a client-server game works with SFML:

1. **Server Initialization:** The game server initializes and sets up game logic, including the game world, player positions, and other relevant data.

2. **Client Initialization:** Players launch the game client, which connects to the server. Each client has a local copy of the game world but relies on the server for authoritative updates.

3. **Networking Loop:** Both the server and clients run networking loops to send and receive messages. SFML's networking module provides classes like `sf::TcpListener` for the server to accept incoming connections and `sf::TcpSocket` for communication with clients.

4. **Game Logic:** Clients send player input (e.g., move commands) to the server, which processes these inputs and updates the game state. The server then broadcasts the updated state to all clients.

5. **Client Rendering:** Clients receive the updated game state from the server and render it locally. This includes rendering player positions, objects, and any other game elements.

SFML Networking Classes

SFML provides several classes to facilitate networking in your games:

- **`sf::TcpListener`:** This class allows the server to listen for incoming TCP connections from clients.

- **`sf::TcpSocket`:** Clients use this class to create TCP sockets for communication with the server.

- **`sf::UdpSocket`:** SFML supports UDP for real-time communication in games. You can use this class to send and receive UDP packets.

- **`sf::Packet`:** SFML's `sf::Packet` class simplifies data serialization and deserialization for network communication. You can use it to send and receive structured data efficiently.

Synchronizing Game State

Synchronizing the game state between the server and clients is crucial for a smooth multiplayer experience. Here are some considerations:

- **Player Input:** Clients send their input (e.g., keyboard, mouse) to the server. The server processes these inputs and updates the game accordingly.

- **Server Authority:** To prevent cheating, the server has the final say in the game state. Clients may predict local actions, but the server's updates override any discrepancies.

- **Frequent Updates:** The server should send frequent updates to clients to ensure that the game remains responsive. SFML's `sf::Clock` can help manage update intervals.

Security and Anti-Cheating Measures

Ensuring the security of your networked game is essential to prevent cheating and protect player data. Some security measures include:

- **Authentication:** Authenticate clients when they connect to the server to ensure they are legitimate players.

- **Data Validation:** Validate all incoming data to prevent malicious actions or data manipulation.

- **Encryption:** Consider encrypting network traffic to protect data from eavesdropping.

- **Server-Side Validation:** Always validate game actions on the server to prevent cheating.

In the following sections, we will delve into code examples and practical implementations of networked gameplay using SFML, demonstrating how to set up both the server and client sides of a simple multiplayer game.

Section 13.3: Security Considerations for Networked Applications

When developing networked applications, security should be a top priority. Whether you're creating an online multiplayer game or a data-sharing application, you must take measures to protect your users and their data. In this section, we'll explore essential security considerations for networked applications built with SFML.

1. Authentication and Authorization

Authentication is the process of verifying the identity of users or devices. In networked applications, it's crucial to ensure that only legitimate users can access your system. Authentication can be achieved through various methods, such as username-password combinations, API keys, or digital certificates. SFML itself doesn't provide authentication mechanisms but can be used alongside other libraries or services to implement secure user authentication.

Authorization, on the other hand, determines what actions or resources authenticated users are allowed to access. It's essential to implement proper authorization checks to prevent unauthorized access to sensitive data or functionalities in your application.

2. Data Validation

Input validation is a critical security measure. All data received from external sources, including user inputs and network communications, must be validated thoroughly. Sanitizing and validating input data can help prevent common security vulnerabilities like SQL injection, cross-site scripting (XSS), and buffer overflows.

SFML's `sf::Packet` class provides a straightforward way to serialize and deserialize data for network communication. However, you should validate the data within these packets to ensure it adheres to expected formats and does not contain malicious payloads.

3. Encryption

Data transmitted over a network can be intercepted by malicious actors if it's not encrypted. Encryption ensures that data remains confidential during transmission. You can implement encryption in your SFML-based networked application using encryption libraries or protocols like Transport Layer Security (TLS) or Secure Socket Layer (SSL).

4. Server-Side Validation

Never trust client-side input or actions. Clients can be compromised or manipulated, so all critical decisions and validations should occur on the server. For example, in a multiplayer game, while clients may predict local actions for responsive gameplay, the server must have the final say on game state to prevent cheating.

5. Rate Limiting and DDoS Mitigation

To protect your networked application from Distributed Denial of Service (DDoS) attacks, consider implementing rate limiting and traffic analysis mechanisms. These measures can help identify and mitigate abnormal traffic patterns and excessive requests from malicious sources.

6. Patch Management

Regularly update your application to address security vulnerabilities and bugs. Keeping all software components, including the SFML library, up-to-date is crucial for maintaining the security of your networked application.

7. Logging and Monitoring

Implement robust logging and monitoring capabilities in your networked application. This allows you to track and analyze network activity, detect unusual behavior, and respond to security incidents promptly.

8. Third-Party Libraries and Dependencies

Be cautious when using third-party libraries and dependencies in your project. Always keep them updated and monitor their security advisories. Vulnerabilities in third-party components can expose your application to security risks.

9. Security Testing

Conduct thorough security testing, including penetration testing and code reviews, to identify vulnerabilities in your networked application. Regular testing can help you discover and address security issues before they can be exploited.

In summary, security is a critical aspect of networked application development. By following best practices, implementing authentication, data validation, encryption, and server-side validation, and staying informed about security threats, you can create networked applications with a strong defense against malicious attacks and ensure the safety of your users and their data.

Section 13.4: Scalability and Load Balancing in Networked Games

Scalability is a crucial consideration for networked games, especially when you anticipate a large number of players connecting to your game servers simultaneously. Load balancing plays a significant role in achieving scalability by distributing incoming network traffic across multiple servers efficiently. In this section, we will explore techniques for ensuring scalability and implementing load balancing in networked games built with SFML.

1. Server Clustering

Server clustering is a common approach to achieve scalability in networked games. In this setup, multiple game servers work together to handle incoming connections and distribute the load evenly. When a player joins the game, they are assigned to one of the available servers within the cluster. This distribution prevents a single server from becoming a bottleneck.

SFML allows you to create multiple server instances that can communicate with each other to synchronize game state and player actions. Implementing a server clustering architecture can be complex but is effective in managing scalability.

2. Load Balancers

Load balancers act as intermediaries between players and game servers. They distribute incoming connections among a pool of servers based on various algorithms, such as round-robin or least-connections. Load balancers can be implemented using dedicated hardware appliances or software solutions.

Popular load balancing software, like Nginx or HAProxy, can be used to distribute player connections to SFML game servers. These tools can also perform health checks on servers to ensure they are responsive and route traffic accordingly.

3. Session Management

In networked games, it's essential to manage player sessions efficiently. Session management involves keeping track of players' connections, game states, and activities. Each server within a cluster must share session information to maintain a consistent game experience for players.

SFML's network capabilities can help in synchronizing player sessions and game state across multiple servers. You can implement a central database or message broker to store and distribute session information.

4. Game State Synchronization

Maintaining consistent game state across multiple servers is a challenge in networked games. When a player's actions affect the game world, all servers must be aware of these changes. You can achieve this through techniques like deterministic lockstep or state replication.

Deterministic lockstep ensures that all servers execute the same game logic in the same order, guaranteeing consistency. State replication involves broadcasting changes in game state to all servers in real-time.

5. Dynamic Scaling

Dynamic scaling allows you to adapt to changing player loads in real-time. When server clusters experience heavy traffic, new servers can be automatically provisioned to handle the increased load. Cloud-based services like Amazon Web Services (AWS) and Google Cloud Platform (GCP) offer auto-scaling features that can be leveraged for dynamic scaling.

SFML-based game servers can be deployed within virtual machines or containers, making it easier to create and destroy server instances as needed.

6. Latency Considerations

When implementing load balancing, consider the impact on player latency. Players should be routed to game servers with low latency to ensure a responsive gaming experience. Load balancers can use geographic location or latency-based routing to achieve this.

In summary, achieving scalability and load balancing in networked games is essential for handling a large number of players while maintaining a seamless gaming experience. Implementing server clustering, load balancers, session management, game state synchronization, dynamic scaling, and latency-aware routing can help you create a robust and scalable networked game infrastructure with SFML.

Section 13.5: Building Cross-Platform Online Multiplayer Games

Creating cross-platform online multiplayer games with SFML requires careful planning and consideration of various factors. In this section, we will explore the steps and best practices for building online multiplayer games that can run seamlessly on different platforms.

1. Networking Libraries and Protocols

Before diving into game development, choose a networking library that supports cross-platform communication. SFML's network module provides the foundation for network communication, but you may need additional libraries or protocols for more advanced features.

Protocols like WebSocket and HTTP can be used for real-time communication between game clients and servers. Libraries like Boost.Asio or ENet can enhance SFML's networking capabilities.

2. Cross-Platform Compatibility

Ensure that your game code is platform-agnostic. Use preprocessor directives or platform-specific code when necessary to handle platform differences. Pay attention to issues like endianness, file path separators, and input device variations.

SFML's platform abstraction helps simplify some of these differences, but thorough testing on each target platform is essential.

3. User Authentication and Security

Implement user authentication and security measures to protect player accounts and data. Use industry-standard practices like secure password hashing, encryption, and token-based authentication. Avoid sending sensitive data in plaintext over the network.

Consider implementing a secure authentication server to centralize user account management and validation.

4. Latency Compensation

Latency can vary significantly between players, affecting gameplay fairness. Implement latency compensation techniques to ensure that all players have a consistent experience. Techniques may include client-side prediction, interpolation, and lag compensation.

5. Server Infrastructure

Select an appropriate hosting solution for your game servers. Cloud platforms like AWS, Azure, or GCP offer scalable and reliable options. Use server instances that match your game's requirements, considering factors like CPU, memory, and network bandwidth.

6. Game State Synchronization

Synchronize game state between clients and servers to maintain consistency. Consider using a dedicated game server that acts as the authoritative source of truth. Clients send player input to the server, which processes it and broadcasts updates to all connected clients.

7. Matchmaking and Lobbies

Implement matchmaking and lobby systems to allow players to find and join games easily. Matchmaking algorithms should consider factors like player skill, latency, and player preferences. Provide options for creating private lobbies for friends to play together.

8. Cross-Platform Voice and Chat

Include voice and text chat features that work across different platforms. Utilize third-party services like Discord or implement your own communication system. Ensure that players can communicate effectively, enhancing the multiplayer experience.

9. Testing and Debugging

Thoroughly test your game on each target platform to identify and fix platform-specific issues. Use debugging tools and profilers to optimize performance and catch any memory leaks or crashes.

10. Post-Release Support

After launching your game, continue to provide support and updates. Listen to player feedback and address issues promptly. Consider adding new content, fixing bugs, and optimizing performance based on player feedback and evolving platform requirements.

Building cross-platform online multiplayer games with SFML can be challenging but rewarding. By considering networking libraries, cross-platform compatibility, security, latency compensation, server infrastructure, game state synchronization, matchmaking, voice and chat, testing, and ongoing support, you can create engaging multiplayer experiences that cater to players on various platforms.

Chapter 14: Cross-Platform Deployment and App Stores

Section 14.1: Preparing Your Application for Deployment

Preparing your application for deployment is a crucial step in the software development process. This section will guide you through the necessary steps to ensure your SFML-based application is ready for deployment on various platforms and app stores.

1. Platform-Specific Considerations

Each platform has its own requirements and guidelines for app deployment. Familiarize yourself with the documentation and guidelines provided by the platform you intend to target (e.g., Windows, macOS, Linux, iOS, Android).

2. Code Signing and Certificates

For platforms like iOS and macOS, code signing is mandatory. Obtain the necessary certificates and provisioning profiles from the respective developer programs (Apple Developer Program, Google Play Console) to sign your application.

3. Dependency Management

Ensure that all external dependencies (SFML, additional libraries) are bundled or installed correctly on the target platform. On some platforms, such as Linux, you may need to provide instructions for users to install dependencies themselves.

4. Build Configurations

Set up different build configurations for each target platform. This may involve adjusting compiler flags, linking to platform-specific libraries, and handling conditional compilation for platform-specific code.

5. Graphics and Resolution

Consider how your application handles different screen resolutions and aspect ratios. Implement responsive design or adaptive layouts to ensure your app looks and functions well on various devices.

6. Performance Optimization

Optimize your application's performance for each platform. Some platforms may have limited resources, so profiling and optimizing your code are essential. Utilize platform-specific profiling tools and best practices.

7. User Interface Adaptation

Adapt your user interface to the platform's design guidelines and conventions. Ensure that your app follows the platform's user interface guidelines for a consistent and familiar user experience.

8. Localization and Internationalization

If your app targets international audiences, support multiple languages and locales. Implement localization and internationalization features to provide a localized user experience.

9. App Store Guidelines

Read and adhere to the guidelines of the app stores you plan to publish your application on. These guidelines cover aspects like content policies, app icons, screenshots, and user reviews.

10. Testing and QA

Thoroughly test your application on each target platform to identify and fix platform-specific issues. Conduct quality assurance testing to ensure your app functions correctly and meets the platform's requirements.

11. Documentation and Support

Provide clear documentation for users, including installation instructions and troubleshooting guides. Set up a support system to address user inquiries and issues promptly.

12. Updates and Maintenance

Plan for regular updates and maintenance to keep your application compatible with evolving platform requirements, fix bugs, and add new features. Respond to user feedback to improve the user experience.

13. Distribution Channels

Consider how you will distribute your application. Options include app stores (e.g., Apple App Store, Google Play Store), third-party app distribution platforms, or direct distribution from your website.

14. Marketing and Promotion

Plan your marketing and promotion strategy to increase your app's visibility and reach a wider audience. Use social media, app store optimization, and other marketing channels to attract users.

Preparing your application for deployment requires careful planning and attention to detail. By following these steps and considering platform-specific requirements, you can ensure a smooth deployment process and provide users with a high-quality cross-platform experience.

Section 14.2: Building Installation Packages for Different Platforms

Once you have prepared your SFML-based application for deployment, the next step is to create installation packages tailored to different platforms. These installation packages are essential for users to install your application on their devices. In this section, we will explore the process of building installation packages for various platforms.

Windows Installation Packages

For Windows, the most common installation package format is the Windows Installer Package (MSI). You can use tools like WiX (Windows Installer XML) to create MSI files for your application. WiX allows you to define installation steps, specify dependencies, and customize the installation process.

Here is an example of a basic WiX script to create an MSI installer:

```
<?xml version="1.0" encoding="UTF-8"?>
<Wix xmlns="http://schemas.microsoft.com/wix/2006/wi">
  <Product Id="*" Name="MySFMLApp" Language="1033" Version="1.0.0.0" Manufact
urer="YourCompany" UpgradeCode="PUT-GUID-HERE">
    <Package InstallerVersion="200" Compressed="yes" InstallScope="perMachine
" />

    <MajorUpgrade DowngradeErrorMessage="A newer version of MySFMLApp is alre
ady installed." />

    <Media Id="1" Cabinet="MySFMLApp.cab" EmbedCab="yes" />

    <Feature Id="ProductFeature" Title="MySFMLApp" Level="1">
      <ComponentRef Id="MainExecutable" />
    </Feature>

    <Directory Id="TARGETDIR" Name="SourceDir">
      <Directory Id="ProgramFilesFolder">
        <Directory Id="INSTALLFOLDER" Name="MySFMLApp" />
      </Directory>
    </Directory>

    <Component Id="MainExecutable" Guid="PUT-GUID-HERE">
      <File Id="MySFMLAppEXE" Source="path\to\your\application.exe" KeyPath="
yes" />
    </Component>
  </Product>
</Wix>
```

macOS Installation Packages

On macOS, package distribution is commonly done using disk images (DMG files) or macOS application bundles. To create a DMG file, you can use tools like `hdiutil` and `create-dmg`. This allows you to package your application with a user-friendly drag-and-drop installation process.

Here's an example command to create a DMG file using `create-dmg`:

```
create-dmg 'path/to/your/application.app' --overwrite
```

Linux Installation Packages

Linux distributions use various package managers like APT, RPM, or Snap for software installation. To distribute your application on Linux, you should create packages in the format required by the target distribution.

For example, on Debian-based systems (e.g., Ubuntu), you can create a DEB package using tools like `dpkg` and `debhelper`. On Red Hat-based systems (e.g., Fedora), you can build RPM packages with `rpmbuild` and `rpmlint`. Snaps are another distribution format that provides cross-distribution compatibility.

Each distribution has its own packaging guidelines, so be sure to consult the documentation and guidelines for the specific distribution you are targeting.

Cross-Platform Packaging

To simplify cross-platform packaging, consider using packaging tools like CPack, which is a part of CMake (a popular build system). CPack allows you to create installation packages for multiple platforms from a single project configuration.

Here's an example of using CPack in a CMakeLists.txt file:

```
include(CPack)

set(CPACK_PACKAGE_NAME "MySFMLApp")
set(CPACK_PACKAGE_VERSION "1.0.0")
set(CPACK_GENERATOR "ZIP;TGZ;DEB;RPM;NSIS")
set(CPACK_PACKAGE_VENDOR "YourCompany")

include(CPack)
```

By configuring CPack, you can create installation packages for Windows (NSIS), Linux (DEB and RPM), and macOS (ZIP and TGZ) all in one go.

Building installation packages is an essential part of software deployment, as it simplifies the installation process for end-users and ensures that your application can be easily distributed and installed on various platforms. Remember to follow platform-specific guidelines and best practices to create packages that are reliable and user-friendly.

Section 14.3: Distributing Your App on iOS and Android Stores

Distributing your application on iOS and Android requires adherence to platform-specific requirements and guidelines. In this section, we'll explore the process of preparing and distributing your SFML-based application on the iOS App Store and the Google Play Store.

iOS App Store Distribution

1. Apple Developer Program Enrollment

Before you can distribute your app on the iOS App Store, you must enroll in the Apple Developer Program. This program provides you with the necessary tools and resources for iOS app development and distribution.

2. Xcode and iOS Development

To develop and distribute iOS apps, you'll need Xcode, Apple's integrated development environment (IDE). You'll also need to set up your development environment to target iOS devices.

3. Code Signing and Provisioning Profiles

Apple requires code signing for iOS apps to ensure their authenticity. You'll need to create provisioning profiles and certificates through the Apple Developer Portal. These profiles link your app to specific iOS devices and enable distribution through the App Store.

4. App Store Connect

App Store Connect is Apple's platform for managing app submissions, app versions, and metadata. You'll use it to prepare your app for distribution and submit it for review.

5. App Submission and Review

To submit your app to the App Store, provide detailed information about your app, including screenshots, descriptions, and pricing. Apple will review your app for compliance with their guidelines. Once approved, your app will be available on the App Store for download by users.

Google Play Store Distribution

1. Google Play Console Registration

To distribute your Android app on the Google Play Store, you need to create a developer account on the Google Play Console. This account comes with a one-time registration fee.

2. Android Development

Android app development requires the Android Studio IDE. You'll use it to create, test, and package your SFML-based app for distribution on Android.

Google Play uses app signing keys to verify the authenticity of Android apps. You can either use the app signing key provided by Google or use your upload key. The key choice affects how you manage your app's signing and updates.

4. Google Play Console

The Google Play Console is your hub for app management. Here, you can upload app bundles or APKs, define app metadata, set pricing, and configure distribution options.

5. App Publishing

Before publishing your app on the Play Store, you'll need to fill out detailed store listings, including app descriptions, screenshots, and promotional graphics. Google also performs a review process to ensure compliance with their policies.

6. App Release and Updates

Google Play allows you to release apps in various tracks, such as production, beta, and alpha. This enables staged rollouts and testing before releasing updates to all users.

Cross-Platform Considerations

When distributing on iOS and Android, keep in mind that SFML is primarily a C++ library. To integrate your SFML-based game or application into these platforms, you may need to write platform-specific code for handling app lifecycle, user interfaces, and other platform-specific features.

Additionally, both Apple and Google have strict guidelines for app content, behavior, and user privacy. Ensure that your SFML application complies with these guidelines to avoid rejection or removal from the app stores.

By following the respective platform guidelines and using the tools provided by Apple and Google, you can successfully distribute your SFML-based application to a wide audience on iOS and Android devices.

Section 14.4: App Store Guidelines and Submission Process

Submitting your app to the iOS App Store or the Google Play Store involves adhering to their respective guidelines and navigating a submission process. In this section, we'll delve into the specifics of these guidelines and the steps required for submitting your SFML-based app.

iOS App Store Guidelines

1. Content Guidelines

Apple maintains strict content guidelines for apps distributed on the App Store. These guidelines cover a wide range of topics, including acceptable content, intellectual property, violence, and more. Ensure your app complies with these guidelines to avoid rejection during the review process.

2. User Interface Design

Apple places a strong emphasis on user interface (UI) design. Your app should provide an intuitive and user-friendly experience, following Apple's Human Interface Guidelines (HIG). Pay attention to app layout, navigation, and interactions to create a seamless user experience.

3. Privacy and Data Security

Apple prioritizes user privacy and data security. You must clearly communicate your app's data collection and usage practices to users and obtain their consent when required. Implement strong security measures to protect user data.

4. Performance and Stability

Apps on the App Store must be stable and perform well. Test your SFML-based app thoroughly to ensure it doesn't crash or exhibit excessive lag. Monitor memory usage and optimize performance to provide a smooth user experience.

5. In-App Purchases

If your app offers in-app purchases, follow Apple's guidelines for implementing them. Clearly communicate pricing and terms to users, and ensure that the purchase process is straightforward and reliable.

6. App Store Review Process

After submitting your app, it undergoes a review process by Apple. This process checks for compliance with guidelines, app functionality, and quality. Be prepared for feedback and, if necessary, make the required adjustments before resubmitting your app.

Google Play Store Guidelines

1. Content Policies

Google Play Store has content policies that govern the type of content allowed in apps. Ensure your SFML app complies with these policies, including restrictions on harmful content, sensitive information, and intellectual property.

2. User Interface and User Experience

Similar to Apple, Google emphasizes good UI and UX design. Follow the Material Design guidelines to create a visually appealing and user-friendly app. Optimize your app for different screen sizes and orientations.

3. Permissions and Data Handling

Request only the permissions necessary for your app's functionality, and explain to users why you need them. Handle user data with care, and obtain explicit consent for data collection, especially for sensitive information.

4. Performance and Stability

Google expects apps to be stable and responsive. Thoroughly test your SFML-based app to ensure it functions well on various Android devices. Address any crashes or performance issues before submission.

5. In-App Purchases and Billing

If your app offers in-app purchases, use Google Play Billing for transactions. Follow Google's guidelines for pricing, billing, and refunds. Clearly communicate pricing to users, and ensure they receive what they've paid for.

6. Google Play Console and Submission

Use the Google Play Console to submit your app. Fill out detailed app listings, including descriptions, screenshots, and promotional materials. Google will review your app to verify compliance with their policies.

Tips for Successful Submission

1. **Thorough Testing**: Before submission, conduct extensive testing on real devices to identify and fix any issues.

2. **Appropriate Content**: Ensure your app's content is suitable for all audiences and doesn't violate guidelines.

3. **Privacy Policy**: Include a clear and easily accessible privacy policy in your app, detailing data handling practices.

4. **Support and Updates**: Be prepared to provide customer support and release updates to address issues and improve your app.

5. **Prompt Response**: Respond promptly to any communication from Apple or Google during the review process.

By carefully following the guidelines and best practices of the respective app stores, you can increase the chances of your SFML-based app being accepted and made available to a wide audience.

Section 14.5: Post-Release Support and Updates

Launching your SFML-based application on app stores is a significant milestone, but it's not the end of your journey. Post-release support and updates are crucial for maintaining and improving your app's performance, fixing bugs, and adding new features. In this section, we'll explore the importance of post-release support and how to effectively manage it.

The Importance of Post-Release Support

1. **Bug Fixes**: Users may encounter bugs or issues with your app after its release. Providing prompt bug fixes enhances user satisfaction and prevents negative reviews.

2. **Compatibility Updates**: As mobile platforms and devices evolve, your app may face compatibility issues. Regular updates ensure your app works smoothly on the latest operating systems and hardware.

3. **Security Patches**: Security vulnerabilities can emerge over time. Staying vigilant and addressing security concerns with updates is crucial for protecting user data.

4. **User Feedback**: Listen to user feedback and use it to make improvements. Users often provide valuable insights that can lead to a better user experience.

5. **New Features**: To keep users engaged and attract new ones, consider adding new features and enhancements. This can also differentiate your app from competitors.

Managing Post-Release Updates

1. **Update Planning**: Establish a clear plan for updates, including bug-fixing releases, feature updates, and major version releases. Consider a regular release schedule to keep users engaged.

2. **Bug Tracking**: Use bug-tracking tools to efficiently manage and prioritize reported issues. Assign tasks to developers and maintain a record of bug fixes.

3. **Version Control**: Use version control systems like Git to manage your app's source code. This helps track changes and collaborate with team members.

4. **Testing**: Rigorous testing is essential before each update to ensure that new features work as intended and that existing functionality remains stable.

5. **Backward Compatibility**: While adding new features, ensure backward compatibility to avoid breaking functionality for existing users.

6. **User Communication**: Keep users informed about updates through release notes. Explain what's new, what issues were fixed, and how the update benefits them.

7. **User Feedback Channels**: Maintain channels for users to provide feedback and report issues. Encourage open communication to foster a positive user-community relationship.

8. **Data Backups**: If your app stores user data, implement data backup mechanisms. This safeguards user data during updates or in case of unforeseen issues.

9. **A/B Testing**: Experiment with new features or changes on a smaller subset of users before rolling them out to the entire user base.

App Store Update Process

1. **Submission**: Prepare and test your update thoroughly before submission. Ensure it complies with app store guidelines.

2. **Review Process**: Both Apple and Google review updates to ensure they adhere to their guidelines. Be prepared for possible feedback and revisions.

3. **Deployment**: Once approved, your update is deployed to users. This process can take several hours to propagate to all users.

4. **User Notification**: Users receive notifications about available updates, and they can choose to install them.

5. **Monitoring**: After an update, monitor user feedback and app performance to catch any unexpected issues that may have arisen.

6. **Iterate**: Use user feedback and app analytics to inform future updates and improvements.

Remember that maintaining a positive relationship with your user base is vital. Address negative reviews and user complaints promptly and professionally. Continuous improvement and engagement can lead to long-term success for your SFML-based app in the competitive app marketplace.

Chapter 15: Advanced Debugging and Profiling Techniques

In this chapter, we dive into advanced debugging and profiling techniques for SFML-based applications. Debugging and profiling are critical aspects of software development, helping you identify and resolve issues and optimize your code. In this chapter, we will explore advanced tools and strategies to improve your debugging and profiling skills.

Section 15.1: Advanced Debugging Tools and Strategies

In Section 15.1, we'll explore advanced debugging tools and strategies that go beyond basic breakpoints and print statements. We'll look at techniques for debugging multithreaded applications, debugging remotely, and using advanced debugging features offered by integrated development environments (IDEs).

Section 15.2: Profiling and Performance Optimization

Section 15.2 focuses on profiling and performance optimization. Profiling tools help you identify bottlenecks and performance issues in your code. We'll discuss how to use profilers effectively and interpret their output. Additionally, we'll explore strategies for optimizing your code to achieve better performance.

Section 15.3: Memory Leak Detection and Prevention

Memory leaks can be a significant source of problems in long-running applications. In Section 15.3, we'll dive into memory leak detection techniques. We'll explore tools and strategies for identifying memory leaks and discuss best practices for preventing them in your SFML applications.

Section 15.4: Advanced Debugging for Multi-Platform Applications

Developing cross-platform applications comes with its own set of debugging challenges. In Section 15.4, we'll address advanced debugging techniques specific to multi-platform development. We'll discuss strategies for handling platform-specific issues and debugging on different operating systems.

Section 15.5: Troubleshooting Cross-Platform Challenges

In Section 15.5, we'll focus on troubleshooting common cross-platform challenges that developers face when working with SFML. We'll cover issues related to differences in compiler and library versions, handling platform-specific dependencies, and resolving cross-platform compatibility problems.

Advanced debugging and profiling skills are invaluable for delivering high-quality, performant software. Whether you're developing games, multimedia applications, or other software with SFML, this chapter will equip you with the knowledge and tools to tackle complex debugging and optimization tasks effectively.

Chapter 15: Advanced Debugging and Profiling Techniques

Section 15.1: Advanced Debugging Tools and Strategies

In this section, we'll delve into advanced debugging tools and strategies that can significantly enhance your ability to diagnose and resolve issues in your SFML-based applications. While basic debugging techniques like setting breakpoints and printing variables are essential, complex applications often require more sophisticated approaches.

1. Remote Debugging

Remote debugging is a powerful technique that allows you to debug an application running on a different machine or environment. It's particularly useful for debugging cross-platform applications or applications deployed on remote servers. Many integrated development environments (IDEs) support remote debugging.

To enable remote debugging, you typically need to:

- Start your application in a debuggable mode, often by adding command-line options.
- Configure your IDE to connect to the remote debugging session, specifying the host and port where your application is running.

2. Multithreaded Debugging

Multithreaded applications can be challenging to debug due to the concurrent execution of multiple threads. Advanced debugging tools offer features to help you understand and control thread interactions. These tools allow you to set thread-specific breakpoints, inspect thread-specific variables, and visualize thread execution.

3. Conditional Breakpoints

Conditional breakpoints are breakpoints that only trigger when a specified condition is met. This can be incredibly useful for narrowing down issues in complex loops or when you want to break execution when a specific variable reaches a certain value. Most modern IDEs support conditional breakpoints, allowing you to specify conditions using the programming language's expressions.

Here's an example in C++ using the GDB debugger:

```
for (int i = 0; i < 100; ++i) {
    // ...
    if (i == 42) {
        // Break only when i equals 42
        int breakpoint_here = 0; // Place a breakpoint here
    }
    // ...
}
```

4. Advanced Profiling Integration

Some debugging tools integrate with profiling data, allowing you to analyze performance-related issues while debugging. This can be immensely helpful when you suspect that a performance problem is related to a specific code section. Profiling data can provide insights into CPU and memory usage, helping you pinpoint bottlenecks.

5. Postmortem Debugging

Postmortem debugging involves analyzing crash dumps or core dumps generated when an application crashes. Advanced debugging tools and symbol files can be used to inspect the state of the application at the time of the crash, even if the crash occurred on a user's machine.

Advanced debugging tools like GDB and LLDB provide extensive features for analyzing crash dumps and core dumps.

Incorporating these advanced debugging techniques into your development workflow can save you time and effort when diagnosing and resolving complex issues in your SFML applications. While basic debugging methods remain essential, having these advanced tools and strategies in your toolkit can make a significant difference in your debugging efficiency.

Section 15.2: Profiling and Performance Optimization

In this section, we'll explore the essential aspects of profiling and performance optimization in SFML applications. Profiling is the process of analyzing the execution of your code to identify bottlenecks, memory leaks, or other performance issues. By optimizing your code based on profiling results, you can significantly improve your application's performance.

Profiling Tools

Profiling tools are essential for identifying performance bottlenecks in your SFML applications. Some popular profiling tools include:

1. **Valgrind:** Valgrind is a powerful tool for memory analysis. It can detect memory leaks, heap and stack memory errors, and provide performance profiling. Using Valgrind with your SFML application can help you identify memory-related issues.

2. **gprof:** The GNU Profiler (gprof) is a command-line profiling tool for GNU-based applications. It provides insights into which functions are consuming the most CPU time. To use gprof, you'll need to compile your SFML application with the `-pg` compiler flag and then run it to generate profiling data.

3. **Perf:** Perf is a performance analysis tool that comes with the Linux kernel. It provides various profiling capabilities, including CPU and memory profiling. Perf can help you identify CPU hotspots and analyze memory usage.

4. **SFML Profiler:** SFML itself provides a simple profiling tool that allows you to measure the time taken by specific code sections. You can use `sf::Clock` or `sf::Time` to measure time intervals and identify performance bottlenecks within your SFML code.

Profiling Workflow

Here's a typical workflow for profiling your SFML application:

1. **Instrument Your Code:** To begin profiling, you need to instrument your code by adding profiling code or using profiling tools like Valgrind or gprof. Profiling code can involve measuring the time spent in specific functions or tracking memory allocations and deallocations.

2. **Run the Profiler:** Execute your instrumented SFML application under the profiler of your choice. This will collect data about the application's runtime behavior.

3. **Analyze Profiling Data:** After running the application, analyze the profiling data generated by the profiler. Look for functions or code sections that consume a significant amount of CPU time or exhibit memory-related issues.

4. **Optimize the Code:** Based on the profiling results, optimize the identified bottlenecks. This may involve algorithmic improvements, reducing memory allocations, or parallelizing code to better utilize multiple CPU cores.

5. **Repeat the Process:** Profiling and optimization are often iterative processes. After making changes to your code, rerun the profiler to validate the improvements. Continue this process until you achieve the desired performance gains.

Memory Profiling

Memory profiling is crucial for identifying memory leaks and excessive memory usage in your SFML applications. Tools like Valgrind can help you detect memory-related issues by tracking memory allocations and deallocations. When using Valgrind, focus on resolving memory leaks, invalid read or write operations, and heap-related errors.

CPU Profiling

CPU profiling helps identify functions or code sections that consume a significant amount of CPU time. Gprof and Perf can be valuable tools for CPU profiling. Look for functions with high CPU usage and consider optimizing them. Profiling can reveal hotspots in your code, such as loops or rendering operations, that may benefit from optimization.

Conclusion

Profiling and performance optimization are critical aspects of SFML application development. By using profiling tools and following a systematic profiling workflow, you can identify and resolve performance bottlenecks and memory-related issues in your applications. Profiling not only helps ensure that your SFML applications run smoothly but also provides insights into how to make them more efficient and responsive.

Section 15.3: Memory Leak Detection and Prevention

Memory leaks are a common issue in software development, including SFML applications. A memory leak occurs when a program allocates memory but fails to release it when it's no longer needed. Over time, these unreleased memory blocks can accumulate, causing the program's memory consumption to grow indefinitely and potentially leading to crashes or degraded performance. In this section, we'll explore memory leak detection and prevention techniques for SFML applications.

Detecting Memory Leaks

Detecting memory leaks is the first step in addressing this issue. Here are some tools and techniques you can use to identify memory leaks in your SFML application:

1. **Valgrind:** Valgrind is a widely-used memory analysis tool that can detect memory leaks. Running your SFML application through Valgrind's `memcheck` tool will highlight memory allocations that were not deallocated properly.

2. **SFML's Memory Leak Detection:** SFML provides a simple memory leak detection feature that can help you identify memory leaks specific to SFML resources like textures, fonts, and sounds. You can enable this feature by defining the `SFML_DEBUG` macro before including SFML headers.

```
#define SFML_DEBUG
#include <SFML/Graphics.hpp>
```

3. **Custom Logging:** You can implement custom logging of memory allocations and deallocations in your code to track resource creation and destruction. By comparing the counts of allocations and deallocations, you can detect potential memory leaks.

Memory Leak Prevention

Once you've detected memory leaks, it's essential to prevent them. Here are some best practices for memory leak prevention in SFML applications:

1. **Resource Management:** Use smart pointers or resource management classes to handle SFML resources like textures, fonts, and sounds. When these objects go out of scope, their destructors will automatically release associated resources.

2. **Scope and Lifetime:** Be mindful of the scope and lifetime of objects that manage SFML resources. Ensure that resources are released when they are no longer needed, especially in functions and classes where resource management is critical.

3. **Use Containers:** When managing collections of resources, consider using standard containers like `std::vector` or `std::unordered_map` along with smart pointers to store and manage SFML resources. This ensures proper resource cleanup when the container goes out of scope.

4. **Debugging and Testing:** Regularly test your SFML application for memory leaks, especially after making significant changes. Tools like Valgrind and SFML's memory leak detection can help you catch memory issues early in development.

Best Practices for Memory Management

In addition to memory leak prevention, adopting best practices for memory management in your SFML application can help maintain good memory hygiene:

1. **Resource Pools:** Implement resource pools for frequently created and destroyed objects, such as bullets in a game. Recycling objects from a pool can reduce memory fragmentation.

2. **Minimize Dynamic Allocation:** Avoid excessive dynamic memory allocation and deallocation during runtime. Prefer stack allocation or resource reuse whenever possible.

3. **Profiling:** Regularly profile your application to identify memory usage patterns and optimize resource allocation and deallocation accordingly.

4. **Documentation:** Document memory management practices and ownership rules for SFML resources in your codebase to ensure consistency among team members.

By adopting these memory leak detection and prevention techniques and following best practices for memory management, you can create stable and efficient SFML applications that minimize memory-related issues and deliver a smooth user experience.

Section 15.4: Advanced Debugging for Multi-Platform Applications

Debugging multi-platform applications can be a challenging task due to the inherent differences between various platforms, compilers, and libraries. In this section, we'll explore advanced debugging techniques and tools to help you diagnose and resolve issues in your multi-platform SFML applications effectively.

Cross-Platform Debugging Challenges

Multi-platform applications often face platform-specific challenges that can be difficult to diagnose. These challenges may include:

1. **Compiler and Library Differences:** Each platform may use different compilers and library versions, leading to compatibility issues.

2. **Resource Path Handling:** File and resource path handling can vary between platforms, causing errors related to loading assets.

3. **Platform-Specific Bugs:** Bugs that manifest only on specific platforms can be challenging to reproduce and debug.

Advanced Debugging Tools

To address these challenges, consider using the following advanced debugging tools and techniques:

1. **Cross-Platform Development Environments:** Utilize integrated development environments (IDEs) and build systems that support multi-platform development, such as CMake. These tools can help manage platform-specific configurations and build scripts.

2. **Conditional Compilation:** Use preprocessor directives to conditionally compile code for different platforms. For example, you can use `#ifdef` directives to isolate platform-specific code sections and address platform-specific issues.

```
#ifdef _WIN32
    // Windows-specific code
#elif __linux__
    // Linux-specific code
#elif __APPLE__
    // macOS-specific code
#endif
```

3. **Cross-Platform Debugging Tools:** IDEs like Visual Studio, CLion, and Xcode provide cross-platform debugging support. They allow you to set breakpoints, inspect variables, and step through code on different platforms.

4. **Remote Debugging:** For platforms without a native development environment, consider remote debugging. Tools like GDB (GNU Debugger) can be used to debug applications running on remote devices or platforms.

5. **Version Control and Continuous Integration:** Use version control systems like Git and CI/CD pipelines to automate the testing and debugging of your multi-platform application on different platforms.

Logging and Tracing

Logging and tracing are invaluable for diagnosing issues in multi-platform applications. Implement comprehensive logging and tracing mechanisms in your code to record the application's behavior across platforms. Consider the following best practices:

1. **Log Levels:** Use different log levels (e.g., debug, info, warning, error) to categorize log messages. This allows you to filter and focus on relevant information during debugging.

2. **Platform Identification:** Include platform identification information in log messages to differentiate between platform-specific behavior.

3. **Timestamps:** Include timestamps in log messages to correlate events across platforms and track the sequence of actions leading to an issue.

4. **Verbose Mode:** Implement a verbose mode that provides detailed logging for debugging purposes. This can be enabled or disabled as needed.

```
bool verboseMode = false;

void LogDebug(const std::string& message) {
    if (verboseMode) {
        // Log the debug message
    }
}
```

Crash Reporting and Error Handling

In addition to logging, implement robust error handling and crash reporting mechanisms in your multi-platform application. Capture crash dumps and error reports to diagnose issues that result in application crashes. Services like Crashlytics and Sentry can help automate crash reporting across platforms.

By combining these advanced debugging tools and techniques with thorough testing on each target platform, you can effectively diagnose and resolve issues in your multi-platform SFML applications, ensuring a reliable and consistent user experience across diverse environments.

Section 15.5: Troubleshooting Cross-Platform Challenges

Troubleshooting cross-platform challenges is a crucial aspect of developing multi-platform SFML applications. In this section, we'll explore strategies and common issues encountered during cross-platform development and how to overcome them.

Common Cross-Platform Challenges

1. **Platform-Specific Behavior:** Different platforms may have platform-specific behaviors, bugs, or limitations. It's essential to identify and address these differences to ensure a consistent user experience.

2. **Compiler and Library Compatibility:** Compilers and library versions can vary across platforms. Incompatibilities may lead to build errors or runtime issues. Maintaining compatibility or providing platform-specific workarounds is key.

3. **Resource Management:** File paths, resource loading, and file system behavior can differ. Ensure consistent resource management by using platform-independent methods or handling platform-specific cases.

4. **Input Handling:** Input devices (e.g., keyboards, mice, touchscreens) can have platform-specific characteristics. Consider using SFML's input handling to abstract these differences.

Strategies for Troubleshooting

1. Logging and Debugging

Implement extensive logging throughout your application to trace execution and capture relevant information. Log platform-specific details to identify and diagnose issues unique to each platform.

```
void LogPlatformDetails() {
    #ifdef _WIN32
        Log("Running on Windows");
    #elif __linux__
        Log("Running on Linux");
```

```
    #elif __APPLE__
        Log("Running on macOS");
    #endif
}
```

Leverage debugging tools provided by your development environment, such as breakpoints, variable inspection, and call stack tracing. Test your application on each platform, and if an issue arises, use debugging to pinpoint its source.

2. Cross-Platform Testing

Regularly test your application on all target platforms to catch platform-specific issues early. Automated testing and continuous integration can help streamline this process. Services like Travis CI and Jenkins support multi-platform testing.

3. Isolating Platform-Specific Code

Use preprocessor directives (#ifdef) to isolate platform-specific code blocks. This allows you to address platform-specific issues without affecting other platforms.

```
#ifdef _WIN32
    // Windows-specific code
#elif __linux__
    // Linux-specific code
#elif __APPLE__
    // macOS-specific code
#endif
```

4. Version Control and Issue Tracking

Maintain a version control system (e.g., Git) to track changes across platforms. Create platform-specific branches or tags to manage platform-specific code.

Use issue tracking systems (e.g., Jira, GitHub Issues) to document and prioritize platform-specific issues and track their resolution.

5. Cross-Platform Libraries

Consider using cross-platform libraries and tools to minimize platform-specific challenges. Libraries like Boost and Qt provide cross-platform solutions for various tasks, including threading, file I/O, and user interface development.

6. User Community and Forums

Engage with the SFML user community and online forums. Other developers may have encountered and solved similar cross-platform issues. Sharing experiences and seeking advice can be valuable.

7. Documentation and Knowledge Sharing

Maintain detailed documentation about your cross-platform development process, including platform-specific workarounds and solutions. Share this knowledge with your development team and the broader community.

8. Keep Up with Updates

Stay informed about updates and changes in the SFML library, compilers, and platforms. Updating to the latest versions can resolve compatibility issues and improve performance.

9. Embrace Cross-Platform Principles

Follow cross-platform development principles from the beginning of your project. This includes using platform-independent APIs, modular code design, and handling platform-specific cases gracefully.

By applying these strategies and addressing common challenges, you can troubleshoot cross-platform issues effectively and create robust and reliable multi-platform SFML applications. Troubleshooting is an essential part of the development process, ensuring that your application delivers a consistent and high-quality experience on various platforms.

Chapter 16: Beyond SFML: Exploring Alternative Libraries and Frameworks

In this chapter, we'll venture beyond SFML and explore alternative libraries and frameworks for multimedia programming. While SFML is a powerful and versatile library, there are other options available that may better suit specific project requirements or provide additional features.

Section 16.1: Overview of Alternative Multimedia Libraries

Before we dive into specific alternatives, let's take an overview of some alternative multimedia libraries commonly used in the industry. Each of these libraries has its unique strengths and use cases.

1. SDL (Simple DirectMedia Layer)

SDL is a widely used cross-platform multimedia library that provides low-level access to audio, keyboard, mouse, joystick, and graphics hardware via OpenGL and Direct3D. It is known for its simplicity and portability, making it a good choice for game development and multimedia applications.

2. OpenGL

OpenGL is not a library but a cross-platform API for rendering 2D and 3D graphics. It is used for high-performance graphics applications and is often used in combination with other libraries like GLFW and GLEW.

3. SFML Alternatives

SFML has alternatives like Allegro and ClanLib, which offer similar functionality but with different design philosophies and features. Depending on your project's needs, one of these alternatives may be a better fit.

4. Love2D

Love2D is a framework for creating 2D games in the Lua programming language. It is simple and easy to learn, making it a popular choice for indie game developers.

5. Godot Engine

Godot is a powerful open-source game engine that supports 2D and 3D game development. It has a visual editor and a scripting language, making it suitable for both beginners and experienced developers.

6. Unity

Unity is a widely used game development engine that supports 2D and 3D graphics. While it has a steeper learning curve, it offers a wide range of features and is suitable for both indie and AAA game development.

7. Unreal Engine

Unreal Engine is a high-end game engine used in the development of many AAA games. It provides powerful graphics capabilities, but its complexity and resource requirements may not be suitable for all projects.

8. Web-Based Technologies

For web-based multimedia applications, technologies like HTML5, WebGL, and WebAssembly can be used. These technologies leverage web browsers for multimedia rendering and are platform-independent.

9. Audio Libraries

For audio-focused projects, libraries like FMOD and Wwise offer advanced audio features and are commonly used in the gaming industry.

10. Machine Learning Frameworks

If your project involves machine learning or AI, libraries like TensorFlow, PyTorch, and scikit-learn provide comprehensive tools for AI development.

In the following sections, we will delve deeper into some of these alternatives, exploring how they compare to SFML and when to consider using them for your multimedia programming projects. Keep in mind that the choice of library or framework should align with your project's goals, requirements, and your familiarity with the technology involved.

Section 16.2: Integrating Alternative Libraries with SFML

While exploring alternative libraries and frameworks for multimedia programming, it's important to understand that you can often integrate them with SFML to leverage the strengths of both worlds. This section will focus on how to integrate alternative libraries and tools with SFML effectively.

1. SDL Integration

SDL and SFML share similarities in multimedia capabilities. To integrate SDL with SFML, you can use SDL for audio or input handling while still benefiting from SFML's graphics capabilities. This can be especially useful if you have existing SDL-based code and want to migrate to SFML gradually.

Here's an example of how you can use SDL for audio in an SFML project:

```cpp
#include <SFML/Graphics.hpp>
#include <SDL.h>
#include <SDL_audio.h>

// SDL audio callback function
void audioCallback(void* userdata, Uint8* stream, int len) {
    // Fill 'stream' with audio data
    // You can use SDL's audio functions to generate or process audio
}

int main() {
    // Initialize SDL audio subsystem
    if (SDL_Init(SDL_INIT_AUDIO) < 0) {
        // Handle initialization error
        return -1;
    }

    // Create an SFML window
    sf::RenderWindow window(sf::VideoMode(800, 600), "SFML with SDL Audio");

    // Create an SFML sprite or other graphics objects

    // Initialize audio stream with SDL
    SDL_AudioSpec spec;
    spec.callback = audioCallback;
    // Set audio format, sample rate, etc.

    SDL_AudioDeviceID audioDevice = SDL_OpenAudioDevice(nullptr, 0, &spec, nu
llptr, 0);
    if (audioDevice == 0) {
        // Handle audio device error
        return -1;
    }

    SDL_PauseAudioDevice(audioDevice, 0); // Start audio playback

    // SFML game loop
    while (window.isOpen()) {
        // Handle SFML events and update game logic
        // Draw graphics objects

        window.display();
    }

    // Cleanup SDL audio
    SDL_CloseAudioDevice(audioDevice);
    SDL_Quit();
```

```
    return 0;
}
```

2. OpenGL Integration

SFML itself uses OpenGL for rendering, but you can further customize and extend the rendering pipeline by directly working with OpenGL. This is particularly useful when you need advanced 3D rendering capabilities that SFML's high-level abstractions don't provide.

To integrate OpenGL with SFML, you can create an OpenGL context within an SFML window and use OpenGL functions alongside SFML's rendering. Here's a simplified example:

```cpp
#include <SFML/Graphics.hpp>
#include <SFML/OpenGL.hpp>

int main() {
    sf::RenderWindow window(sf::VideoMode(800, 600), "SFML with OpenGL");

    // Create an OpenGL context
    window.setActive();
    glClearColor(0.0f, 0.0f, 0.0f, 1.0f);

    // SFML game loop
    while (window.isOpen()) {
        glClear(GL_COLOR_BUFFER_BIT);

        // Render OpenGL content here

        window.display();
    }

    return 0;
}
```

3. Web-Based Technologies

For web-based multimedia applications, you can use HTML5, WebGL, and JavaScript alongside SFML. Tools like Emscripten allow you to compile C++ code (including SFML-based projects) to WebAssembly, making it compatible with web browsers.

This approach enables you to create cross-platform web games and applications while benefiting from SFML's multimedia features.

4. Machine Learning Integration

If your project involves machine learning, libraries like TensorFlow or PyTorch can be integrated with SFML. You can use SFML for creating the user interface and graphics while using machine learning frameworks for AI-related tasks. This combination is useful for developing interactive applications that utilize AI capabilities.

The key to successful integration is understanding the APIs and capabilities of the libraries you're combining and ensuring they work seamlessly together within your project's architecture. Integrating alternative libraries with SFML can provide you with a powerful toolbox to address various multimedia programming challenges.

Section 16.3: Evaluating the Trade-offs and Benefits

When integrating alternative multimedia libraries and frameworks with SFML, it's essential to carefully evaluate the trade-offs and benefits of such integrations. Every project has its unique requirements and constraints, so understanding the implications of your choices is crucial.

1. Performance Considerations

One of the primary factors to consider is the performance impact of integrating alternative libraries. Some libraries may introduce overhead or require additional resources. For example, integrating a complex physics engine or AI framework may impact your application's performance.

Before making a decision, profile your application and assess its performance with and without the integrated library. Ensure that the performance trade-offs are acceptable for your project's goals.

2. Compatibility and Portability

Another consideration is compatibility and portability. SFML is designed to be cross-platform, and integrating a library that is not equally portable might limit your project's reach. Ensure that the alternative library supports your target platforms and is compatible with SFML's cross-platform capabilities.

3. Development Time and Productivity

Consider how integrating an alternative library impacts your development time and productivity. Some libraries may accelerate development by providing high-level abstractions and pre-built solutions for common tasks. However, they may also introduce complexity and a learning curve.

Evaluate whether the library's features align with your project's requirements and if the benefits outweigh the time spent on integration and learning.

4. Community and Support

The strength of a library's community and the availability of support are crucial factors. Libraries with active communities often receive updates, bug fixes, and community-contributed resources. If you choose a less-supported library, you may face challenges in maintaining and updating your project over time.

5. License and Legal Considerations

Ensure that you understand the licensing terms of any library you integrate into your project. Some libraries may have open-source licenses, while others may have more restrictive terms. Compliance with licensing requirements is essential to avoid legal issues.

6. Scalability and Future-Proofing

Consider your project's long-term scalability and future-proofing. Integrating a library that aligns with your project's growth potential is vital. Assess whether the library can accommodate future feature enhancements or changes in your project's scope.

7. Testing and Quality Assurance

Integrating an alternative library may require additional testing and quality assurance efforts. Ensure that your testing procedures cover the integrated components thoroughly to identify and address any issues promptly.

In conclusion, integrating alternative libraries with SFML can expand your project's capabilities, but it should be a well-considered decision. Evaluate the trade-offs in terms of performance, compatibility, development time, community support, licensing, scalability, and testing. By making informed choices, you can harness the strengths of both SFML and alternative libraries to create robust multimedia applications that meet your project's specific needs.

Section 16.4: Building Cross-Platform Applications with Alternatives

When exploring alternative multimedia libraries and frameworks alongside SFML, you may encounter situations where these alternatives offer unique features or advantages. In this section, we will delve into scenarios where you can leverage these libraries to build cross-platform applications effectively.

1. Specialized Graphics Libraries

Some projects may require specialized graphics capabilities not covered by SFML's core features. In such cases, integrating a graphics library like OpenGL, Vulkan, or DirectX can provide low-level access to hardware rendering capabilities. These libraries can be used in conjunction with SFML to achieve high-performance graphics rendering while maintaining cross-platform compatibility.

```
// Example of integrating OpenGL with SFML
sf::RenderWindow window(sf::VideoMode(800, 600), "SFML with OpenGL");
window.setActive(true);

// Initialize OpenGL
if (glewInit() != GLEW_OK) {
    std::cerr << "GLEW initialization failed!" << std::endl;
    return -1;
```

```
}

// Create and configure OpenGL objects
GLuint vertexArray, vertexBuffer, shaderProgram;
// ... Initialize and bind buffers, compile shaders, etc.

while (window.isOpen()) {
    sf::Event event;
    while (window.pollEvent(event)) {
        if (event.type == sf::Event::Closed)
            window.close();
    }

    // Clear the window
    glClear(GL_COLOR_BUFFER_BIT);

    // Draw OpenGL content here

    // Display the rendered frame
    window.display();
}
```

2. Machine Learning and AI Frameworks

For projects requiring advanced artificial intelligence or machine learning capabilities, integrating dedicated libraries like TensorFlow, PyTorch, or OpenAI Gym can be advantageous. These libraries provide tools for developing AI-driven applications, and by using them in combination with SFML, you can create cross-platform games or simulations with intelligent behaviors.

```
// Example of using TensorFlow with SFML
#include <tensorflow/c/c_api.h>

// Initialize TensorFlow
TF_Graph* graph = TF_NewGraph();
TF_Status* status = TF_NewStatus();
TF_SessionOptions* sessionOpts = TF_NewSessionOptions();
TF_Session* session = TF_NewSession(graph, sessionOpts, status);

// Load a pre-trained model
TF_Buffer* modelData = LoadModel("my_model.pb");
TF_ImportGraphDefOptions* graphOpts = TF_NewImportGraphDefOptions();
TF_GraphImportGraphDef(graph, modelData, graphOpts, status);

// Perform inference
TF_Tensor* inputTensor = CreateInputTensor(inputData);
const TF_Output inputOp = {TF_GraphOperationByName(graph, "input_node"), 0};
TF_Tensor* outputTensor = NULL;
const TF_Output outputOp = {TF_GraphOperationByName(graph, "output_node"), 0}
```

```
;
TF_SessionRun(session, NULL, &inputOp, &inputTensor, 1, &outputOp, &outputTen
sor, 1, NULL, 0, NULL, status);

// Process outputTensor here

// Clean up TensorFlow resources
TF_DeleteGraph(graph);
TF_DeleteSession(session, status);
TF_DeleteSessionOptions(sessionOpts);
TF_DeleteStatus(status);
```

3. Advanced Audio Processing Libraries

When dealing with complex audio processing tasks like real-time analysis, synthesis, or sound spatialization, integrating specialized audio libraries such as PortAudio, JACK, or SuperCollider alongside SFML can be beneficial. These libraries provide extensive audio processing capabilities that can enhance your multimedia applications.

```
// Example of using PortAudio with SFML for audio input
#include <portaudio.h>

// Initialize PortAudio
PaError err = Pa_Initialize();
if (err != paNoError) {
    std::cerr << "PortAudio initialization failed: " << Pa_GetErrorText(err)
<< std::endl;
    return -1;
}

// Set up audio input stream
PaStream* stream;
err = Pa_OpenDefaultStream(&stream, 1, 1, paInt16, 44100, paFramesPerBufferUn
specified, nullptr, nullptr);
if (err != paNoError) {
    std::cerr << "PortAudio stream setup failed: " << Pa_GetErrorText(err) <<
std::endl;
    return -1;
}

err = Pa_StartStream(stream);
if (err != paNoError) {
    std::cerr << "PortAudio stream start failed: " << Pa_GetErrorText(err) <<
std::endl;
    return -1;
}

while (window.isOpen()) {
    // Capture and process audio data from PortAudio stream
```

```
    // Update and render your SFML-based application
}

// Clean up PortAudio resources
Pa_StopStream(stream);
Pa_CloseStream(stream);
Pa_Terminate();
```

4. Augmented Reality and Virtual Reality (AR/VR) Libraries

For AR and VR experiences, integrating AR/VR libraries like ARCore, ARKit, or OpenVR alongside SFML can enable cross-platform development of immersive applications. These libraries provide access to sensors, tracking, and rendering capabilities required for AR and VR.

```
// Example of using ARCore with SFML for augmented reality
#include <arcore_c_api.h>

// Initialize ARCore
ArSession* arSession;
ArSession_create(nullptr, &arSession);

// Set up AR
```

##
Section 16.5: Preparing for Future Multimedia Programming Challenges

As multimedia programming continues to evolve, developers must prepare for future challenges and trends. This section explores key considerations to stay ahead in the dynamic field of multimedia development.

1. **AI and Machine Learning Integration**

The integration of artificial intelligence (AI) and machine learning (ML) will play an increasingly vital role in multimedia applications. Developers should familiarize themselves with ML frameworks like TensorFlow, PyTorch, and scikit-learn to harness the power of AI for tasks such as content recommendation, image recognition, and natural language processing.

```python
# Example of using scikit-learn for machine learning
from sklearn import datasets
from sklearn.model_selection import train_test_split
from sklearn.linear_model import LogisticRegression

# Load a dataset (e.g., Iris dataset)
iris = datasets.load_iris()
X_train, X_test, y_train, y_test = train_test_split(iris.data, iris.target, t
```

```
est_size=0.2, random_state=42)

# Create and train a machine learning model (e.g., logistic regression)
model = LogisticRegression()
model.fit(X_train, y_train)

# Make predictions
predictions = model.predict(X_test)
```

2. 5G and Streaming

The rollout of 5G networks will lead to increased demand for high-quality multimedia streaming. Developers should optimize their applications for faster download and upload speeds, lower latency, and adaptive streaming to ensure a seamless user experience. Leveraging streaming protocols like HTTP Live Streaming (HLS) and Dynamic Adaptive Streaming over HTTP (DASH) will be essential.

```
<!-- Example of using HLS for adaptive streaming -->
<video controls>
    <source src="video.m3u8" type="application/x-mpegURL">
</video>
```

3. Immersive Technologies

Augmented reality (AR) and virtual reality (VR) are poised for growth across various industries. Developers should explore AR/VR development kits like Unity 3D, Unreal Engine, and WebXR to create immersive applications. Additionally, hardware such as AR glasses and VR headsets will become more accessible, offering new possibilities for multimedia experiences.

```
// Example of using Unity 3D for VR development
using UnityEngine;

public class VRMovement : MonoBehaviour
{
    public float speed = 3.0f;

    void Update()
    {
        float horizontal = Input.GetAxis("Horizontal");
        float vertical = Input.GetAxis("Vertical");

        Vector3 movement = new Vector3(horizontal, 0, vertical) * speed * Time.deltaTime;
        transform.Translate(movement);
    }
}
```

4. Security and Privacy

As multimedia applications handle sensitive data, ensuring security and privacy will remain paramount. Developers must implement encryption, secure authentication, and data anonymization techniques. Staying informed about data protection regulations like GDPR and CCPA is essential to avoid legal issues.

```python
# Example of using cryptography library for data encryption
from cryptography.fernet import Fernet

# Generate a secret key
key = Fernet.generate_key()

# Create a Fernet cipher
cipher_suite = Fernet(key)

# Encrypt data
data = b"Sensitive data to encrypt"
cipher_text = cipher_suite.encrypt(data)

# Decrypt data
plain_text = cipher_suite.decrypt(cipher_text)
```

5. Cross-Platform Development

With a growing number of platforms and devices, cross-platform development tools like Flutter, React Native, and Xamarin will become increasingly valuable. These frameworks allow developers to write code once and deploy it on multiple platforms, reducing development time and effort.

```dart
// Example of using Flutter for cross-platform app development
import 'package:flutter/material.dart';

void main() {
  runApp(MyApp());
}

class MyApp extends StatelessWidget {
  @override
  Widget build(BuildContext context) {
    return MaterialApp(
      home: Scaffold(
        appBar: AppBar(
          title: Text('Cross-Platform App'),
        ),
        body: Center(
          child: Text('Hello, World!'),
        ),
      ),
    );
```

```
    }
}
```

In conclusion, staying current with emerging technologies, frameworks, and best practices is crucial for multimedia programmers. By adapting to these trends and challenges, developers can create innovative and successful multimedia applications that cater to the evolving needs of users and industries.

Chapter 17: Advanced Audio Processing

Section 17.1: Real-Time Audio Analysis and Visualization

Real-time audio analysis and visualization are essential techniques in multimedia applications. These capabilities enable developers to create engaging audio-driven experiences, such as music visualizers, voice-controlled applications, and interactive audio effects. In this section, we will explore the fundamentals of real-time audio analysis and visualization.

Understanding Audio Waveforms

Audio waveforms represent the amplitude of sound waves over time. Understanding audio waveforms is crucial for real-time analysis and visualization. Audio data is typically represented as a series of samples, with each sample representing the amplitude of the audio signal at a specific point in time.

```python
# Example: Loading an audio file and plotting its waveform
import librosa
import librosa.display
import matplotlib.pyplot as plt

# Load an audio file
audio_file = "sample.wav"
y, sr = librosa.load(audio_file)

# Plot the audio waveform
plt.figure(figsize=(10, 4))
librosa.display.waveshow(y, sr=sr)
plt.xlabel("Time (s)")
plt.ylabel("Amplitude")
plt.title("Audio Waveform")
plt.show()
```

Real-Time Audio Analysis

Real-time audio analysis involves processing audio data as it is being captured or played back. This analysis can include tasks like pitch detection, beat tracking, and spectral analysis. Libraries like Librosa and Aubio provide tools for real-time audio analysis.

```python
# Example: Real-time pitch detection using Aubio
import aubio

# Initialize Aubio's pitch detection
p = aubio.pitch("default", 2048, 1024, 44100)

# Start the audio stream (replace with your audio source)
# audio_stream = ...
```

```
while True:
    # Read a chunk of audio data from the stream
    # audio_data = ...

    # Perform pitch detection on the audio data
    pitch = p(audio_data)[0]

    # Process the detected pitch (e.g., visualize it)
    # ...

# Close the audio stream when done
# audio_stream.close()
```

Audio Visualization

Audio visualization transforms audio data into graphical representations, providing users with a visual interpretation of sound. Common audio visualizations include waveform displays, spectrograms, and frequency domain representations.

```
# Example: Generating a spectrogram using Librosa
import librosa
import librosa.display
import matplotlib.pyplot as plt

# Load an audio file
audio_file = "sample.wav"
y, sr = librosa.load(audio_file)

# Compute and plot the spectrogram
D = librosa.amplitude_to_db(librosa.stft(y), ref=np.max)
plt.figure(figsize=(10, 4))
librosa.display.specshow(D, sr=sr, x_axis='time', y_axis='log')
plt.colorbar(format='%+2.0f dB')
plt.title('Spectrogram')
plt.show()
```

Real-time audio analysis and visualization open up possibilities for creating interactive and dynamic multimedia applications. Developers can use these techniques to build audio-based games, music production tools, and immersive audio experiences. Understanding the principles behind audio waveforms and utilizing libraries for real-time analysis and visualization are key steps in mastering advanced audio processing.

Section 17.2: Advanced Audio Synthesis Techniques

Advanced audio synthesis techniques are fundamental in creating unique and expressive audio experiences. These techniques allow developers to generate sound in real-time, opening up possibilities for music composition, sound design, and interactive applications. In this section, we'll explore some of the key concepts and methods in advanced audio synthesis.

Understanding Sound Synthesis

Sound synthesis is the process of generating audio signals from scratch or modifying existing ones. It involves creating waveforms, manipulating their properties, and combining them to produce rich and complex sounds. There are several synthesis techniques, each with its own characteristics:

1. **Additive Synthesis:** This technique involves adding multiple sine waves together to create complex sounds. By controlling the frequency, amplitude, and phase of each sine wave, you can generate a wide range of timbres.

2. **Subtractive Synthesis:** Subtractive synthesis starts with a harmonically rich sound source and then filters out unwanted frequencies using filters (e.g., low-pass, high-pass). This process shapes the sound's timbre.

3. **Frequency Modulation (FM) Synthesis:** FM synthesis uses the frequency of one waveform (the modulator) to modulate the frequency of another waveform (the carrier). This creates complex and evolving timbres.

4. **Granular Synthesis:** Granular synthesis breaks audio into tiny grains and plays them back in various ways, often with overlapping and time-stretching. This technique can produce experimental and textured sounds.

5. **Wavetable Synthesis:** Wavetable synthesis involves cycling through a series of pre-recorded waveforms (wavetables) to create evolving timbres. It's commonly used in electronic music.

Implementing Advanced Synthesis in Code

Here's an example of implementing basic additive synthesis in Python using the NumPy library:

```python
import numpy as np
import soundfile as sf

# Sampling parameters
sample_rate = 44100   # Samples per second
duration = 5.0        # Seconds

# Generate a sine wave
frequency = 440.0     # Hertz
t = np.linspace(0, duration, int(sample_rate * duration), endpoint=False)
waveform = 0.5 * np.sin(2 * np.pi * frequency * t)

# Save the waveform as an audio file
sf.write("sine_wave.wav", waveform, sample_rate)
```

Advanced synthesis often involves more complex algorithms and modulation techniques. Libraries like PyDub, FluidSynth, and SuperCollider provide tools and abstractions for various synthesis methods.

Applications of Advanced Synthesis

Advanced audio synthesis techniques find applications in various domains:

- **Music Production:** Musicians use synthesis to create unique sounds, instruments, and effects in music composition and production.

- **Game Audio:** Sound designers use synthesis to generate dynamic and immersive audio environments in games.

- **Interactive Installations:** Artists and developers use real-time synthesis to create interactive installations that respond to user input or environmental factors.

- **Sound Design:** Synthesis is crucial in sound design for film, TV, and multimedia, allowing for the creation of custom sound effects and atmospheres.

Mastering advanced audio synthesis opens up creative avenues for developers and sound designers, enabling them to craft captivating audio experiences and push the boundaries of sonic expression.

Section 17.3: Implementing Sound Spatialization

Sound spatialization is a critical aspect of audio design that enhances immersion and realism in multimedia experiences. It involves positioning audio sources in a virtual space to create a sense of depth and directionality. In this section, we'll explore techniques and concepts for implementing sound spatialization in your projects.

The Importance of Spatial Audio

Spatial audio adds depth and context to soundscapes, making them more engaging for the audience. Whether you're designing a game, virtual reality (VR) experience, or multimedia application, spatialization can greatly enhance the user's perception of the environment.

Imagine a VR game where you hear footsteps approaching from behind, or a movie scene where the sound of rain appears to fall all around you. These immersive experiences are made possible through spatial audio techniques.

Basic Spatialization Techniques

1. **Panning:** The simplest form of spatialization involves panning audio from left to right. This is achieved by adjusting the balance between the left and right speakers. For example, to make a sound appear on the left side, you increase the volume in the left channel.

2. **Distance Attenuation:** Sounds in the real world become quieter as they move farther away. Implementing distance-based volume attenuation is crucial for realistic spatialization. You can use techniques like the inverse square law to calculate the volume drop-off with distance.

3. **Directional Sound:** To create 3D audio experiences, consider the direction from which sounds originate. Techniques like Head-Related Transfer Functions (HRTF) simulate how sounds interact with the listener's ears and head, allowing for precise directional audio.

4. **Reverberation:** Spatial audio isn't just about positioning sounds; it's also about simulating the environment's acoustics. Adding reverb effects can make audio feel like it's in a specific room or space.

Implementing Spatial Audio in Code

Here's a simplified example in Unity (C#) that demonstrates panning audio based on the position of a game object:

```
using UnityEngine;

public class SpatialAudio : MonoBehaviour
{
    public Transform soundSource;
    public AudioSource audioSource;

    void Update()
    {
        if (soundSource != null && audioSource != null)
        {
            Vector3 direction = soundSource.position - transform.position;
            float pan = Mathf.Clamp(direction.x / 10f, -1f, 1f);
            audioSource.panStereo = pan;
        }
    }
}
```

This script adjusts the stereo panning of an `AudioSource` based on the position of a `Transform`. As the sound source moves left or right relative to the listener, the audio's apparent direction changes.

Advanced Spatialization Techniques

For more advanced spatialization, you can explore:

- **Ambisonics:** A higher-order spatial audio technique that captures sound from all directions. It's particularly useful for VR and 360-degree video.

- **Binaural Audio:** Using HRTF-based algorithms, binaural audio simulates how sounds are perceived when they enter the ears from different angles.

- **Doppler Effect:** Simulating the change in frequency (pitch) of a sound as it moves closer or farther away from the listener.

Spatial audio is a broad and evolving field with numerous tools and libraries available to simplify implementation. By mastering spatialization techniques, you can create more immersive and captivating audio experiences in your projects.

Section 17.4: Integrating Voice Recognition and Interaction

Integrating voice recognition and interaction into multimedia applications, games, or even everyday software is becoming increasingly popular. Voice-enabled applications offer a natural and convenient way for users to interact with technology. In this section, we'll explore the integration of voice recognition and interaction into your projects.

The Rise of Voice-Enabled Applications

Voice recognition technology has advanced significantly in recent years, thanks to machine learning and natural language processing techniques. Popular voice assistants like Amazon Alexa, Google Assistant, and Apple Siri have made consumers more comfortable with voice interaction.

Benefits of Voice Interaction

1. **Natural Interaction:** Voice interaction mimics how humans communicate, making it intuitive and user-friendly.

2. **Accessibility:** Voice-enabled applications can benefit users with disabilities or those who prefer spoken commands.

3. **Efficiency:** Voice commands can be faster than manual input for certain tasks.

Voice Recognition Tools and APIs

To integrate voice recognition, you can leverage various tools and APIs:

- **Speech Recognition Libraries:** Many programming languages, such as Python and JavaScript, offer libraries for speech recognition. In Python, the `SpeechRecognition` library is commonly used.

- **Cloud-Based APIs:** Companies like Google, Microsoft, and Amazon provide cloud-based voice recognition APIs, making it easier to implement voice recognition without training your own models.

- **Platform-Specific SDKs:** If you're developing for specific platforms like iOS or Android, you can use platform-specific voice recognition SDKs provided by Apple and Google.

Basic Voice Recognition Example

Here's a simple Python example using the `SpeechRecognition` library:

```python
import speech_recognition as sr

# Initialize recognizer
recognizer = sr.Recognizer()

# Capture audio from the microphone
with sr.Microphone() as source:
    print("Say something:")
    audio = recognizer.listen(source)

try:
    # Recognize the speech
    text = recognizer.recognize_google(audio)
    print("You said:", text)
except sr.UnknownValueError:
    print("Sorry, I could not understand your speech.")
except sr.RequestError as e:
    print("Could not request results; {0}".format(e))
```

This code captures audio from the microphone, sends it to Google's speech recognition service, and prints the recognized text.

Voice-Enabled Applications

Voice recognition can be applied to various use cases:

- **Voice Assistants:** Create your voice assistant with custom commands and responses.

- **Voice-Controlled Games:** Implement voice commands for in-game actions and interactions.

- **Accessibility Features:** Improve accessibility in your software by adding voice navigation and control.

- **Productivity Tools:** Create voice-enabled tools for tasks like note-taking, task management, or language translation.

When integrating voice recognition, consider privacy and user consent. Inform users about data collection and usage to ensure compliance with privacy regulations.

Advanced Voice Interaction

Advanced voice interactions involve natural language processing (NLP), allowing applications to understand context and intent. Implementing NLP typically requires more sophisticated tools and models. Popular NLP libraries like spaCy and NLTK can aid in these endeavors.

In conclusion, voice recognition and interaction open up exciting possibilities for software development. Whether you're building a game, productivity tool, or accessibility feature, voice-enabled applications can enhance user experiences and accessibility. Leveraging readily available tools and APIs can make integrating voice recognition into your projects a relatively straightforward process.

Section 17.5: Audio Processing for Virtual Reality and Augmented Reality

Audio plays a crucial role in creating immersive virtual reality (VR) and augmented reality (AR) experiences. In this section, we'll delve into the significance of audio in VR and AR, and how you can enhance these experiences through audio processing techniques.

The Role of Audio in VR and AR

In VR and AR environments, audio serves several essential functions:

1. **Spatial Awareness:** Audio cues help users understand the spatial layout of the virtual or augmented world. For instance, the sound of footsteps approaching from behind can alert users to potential dangers.

2. **Immersive Atmosphere:** Realistic audio enhances the sense of immersion. It makes virtual worlds feel more believable and engaging.

3. **Interaction Feedback:** Audio can provide feedback when users interact with virtual objects or elements, making the experience more interactive and responsive.

Spatial Audio in VR and AR

Spatial audio is a fundamental concept in VR and AR audio processing. It involves the perception of sound direction and location in a three-dimensional space, mimicking how sound behaves in the real world.

To implement spatial audio, you need to consider:

- **Head-Related Transfer Functions (HRTF):** These functions simulate how sound is altered as it travels from a source to the ears, taking into account the shape of the ears and head. HRTF is crucial for creating realistic audio positioning.

- **Sound Occlusion and Reflection:** Mimicking how sound is blocked or reflected by virtual objects and surfaces contributes to the sense of presence in VR and AR.

Audio Middleware and Engines

Many game engines and audio middleware solutions offer features tailored for VR and AR audio:

- **Unity 3D:** Unity provides a dedicated audio system for VR and AR, including spatial audio features and integration with VR/AR platforms.

- **Unreal Engine:** Unreal Engine offers spatial audio tools and plugins for creating immersive audio experiences.
- **Wwise and FMOD:** Audio middleware like Wwise and FMOD offer spatial audio solutions compatible with VR and AR platforms.

Creating Realistic Soundscapes

To create convincing audio in VR and AR, consider the following techniques:

- **Binaural Audio:** Use binaural recording or synthesis to capture or generate audio that simulates how humans perceive sound in a 3D environment.
- **Ambisonics:** Ambisonic audio is a full-sphere surround sound technique that can provide immersive audio in 360-degree VR experiences.
- **Dynamic Audio:** Implement dynamic audio systems that adjust sounds based on user interactions and the virtual environment. For example, audio should change when a user moves closer to an object or changes their orientation.

Challenges in VR and AR Audio

While VR and AR audio can greatly enhance experiences, they come with challenges:

- **Latency:** Audio must be delivered with minimal latency to match visual and interactive elements.
- **Performance:** Realistic audio processing can be computationally intensive, requiring optimization for smooth performance.
- **Integration:** Seamless integration with VR and AR hardware and platforms is crucial for a consistent user experience.

Conclusion

Audio processing is a vital component of creating immersive and believable VR and AR experiences. Spatial audio, realistic soundscapes, and dynamic audio systems contribute to a sense of presence and engagement for users. Developers should explore the capabilities of audio middleware, engines, and tools specific to VR and AR to ensure audio quality and accuracy in their projects. With careful implementation, audio can elevate VR and AR experiences to new levels of immersion and realism.

Chapter 18: Building a Cross-Platform 2D Animation Studio

Section 18.1: Designing a 2D Animation Project

In this section, we'll explore the process of designing a 2D animation project using SFML and other relevant tools. Building a 2D animation studio involves various steps, from conceptualization to the creation of a functional animation application. We'll outline the key considerations and steps to help you get started.

Understanding the Animation Studio Concept

A 2D animation studio is a software application that enables artists and animators to create 2D animations efficiently. Before diving into development, it's crucial to have a clear understanding of the studio's purpose and target audience. Consider whether it's for professional animators, hobbyists, or educational use. Define the primary features and capabilities you want to include.

Storyboarding and Conceptualization

Storyboarding is a critical phase in any animation project. It involves sketching out the sequence of scenes and frames that make up your animation. At this stage, you'll outline the storyline, characters, and the overall visual style of your animation. Consider creating a user-friendly interface for storyboarding within your animation studio, allowing artists to draw and organize scenes seamlessly.

Timeline and Keyframe Animation

A central component of 2D animation is the timeline. Implement a timeline interface that allows animators to arrange and manipulate keyframes. Keyframes are frames where significant changes in the animation occur. Users should be able to add, remove, and adjust keyframes easily. Consider integrating features for onion skinning, which helps animators see previous and subsequent frames for reference.

Drawing Tools and Layers

Your animation studio should provide a set of drawing tools, including brushes, pencils, and erasers. Implement features for creating and managing layers, similar to professional graphic design software. Layers allow animators to work on different elements of the animation independently, making the process more organized and flexible.

Importing and Exporting Assets

Allow users to import existing images, sprites, and audio files into the animation studio. Provide options for image manipulation and editing. Ensure compatibility with common image formats and consider support for vector graphics to enable scalable animations. Implement export features to save animations in popular video or GIF formats.

Audio Integration

Many animations require sound effects and background music. Integrate audio capabilities, allowing users to import and synchronize audio tracks with their animations. Implement basic audio editing features like volume adjustment, trimming, and looping.

User Interface and UX Design

Design an intuitive and user-friendly interface for your animation studio. Consider the workflow of animators and provide easy access to essential tools and features. Implement keyboard shortcuts and customizable hotkeys to streamline the animation process. Regularly gather user feedback to improve the user experience.

Cross-Platform Considerations

Since this is a cross-platform 2D animation studio, ensure that it runs smoothly on various operating systems, including Windows, macOS, and Linux. Utilize SFML's cross-platform capabilities to achieve this. Test the application on different platforms to identify and resolve any compatibility issues.

Project Management and Collaboration

Consider implementing project management features, allowing users to organize their animations, collaborate with others, and version control their work. Features like cloud storage integration can enhance collaboration and data backup.

Documentation and Tutorials

Provide comprehensive documentation and tutorials within the application to assist users in learning how to use the animation studio effectively. Include tooltips, tooltips, and contextual help to guide users through the interface and features.

In summary, designing a 2D animation studio is a complex but rewarding endeavor. Understanding the needs of animators, creating an intuitive interface, and implementing essential features are key to building a successful animation application. In the following sections, we'll delve deeper into the implementation of specific features and functionalities.

Section 18.2: Implementing Keyframe Animation

In this section, we will focus on the implementation of keyframe animation in your 2D animation studio. Keyframe animation is a fundamental technique used in creating smooth and dynamic animations. Users should be able to define keyframes, set properties for each keyframe, and let the animation software interpolate between these keyframes to create fluid motion.

Keyframes and Animation Properties

Keyframes are frames in the animation where important changes occur. For example, if you are animating the movement of a character across the screen, you might set a keyframe at the starting position and another at the ending position. Users should be able to add keyframes at specific points in the timeline.

Each keyframe should store various animation properties, such as position, scale, rotation, opacity, and any other properties relevant to the animation. When users select a keyframe, they should have the option to edit these properties to create the desired animation effect.

Interpolation Between Keyframes

Interpolation is the process of calculating intermediate frames between keyframes to create smooth transitions. Depending on the type of animation, you may need to implement different interpolation methods:

- **Linear Interpolation:** This is the simplest form of interpolation. It calculates the values between keyframes in a straight-line manner. For example, if you have a keyframe at (0,0) and another at (100,100), linear interpolation will create frames that gradually move the object from (0,0) to (100,100).

- **Bezier Curves:** Bezier curves allow for more complex interpolation, enabling users to create smooth curves and arcs in their animations. Implementing Bezier curve editing tools can be a valuable addition to your animation studio.

Timeline Integration

Integrate the keyframes into the timeline interface. Users should see keyframes represented as markers on the timeline, and they should be able to drag and rearrange these markers to adjust the timing of their animation. Clicking on a keyframe marker should allow users to edit the properties of that keyframe.

Easing Functions

Easing functions control the speed of animation between keyframes. Common easing functions include ease-in, ease-out, and ease-in-out. Allow users to choose or customize easing functions for each keyframe or animation segment.

Onion Skinning

Onion skinning is a technique that allows animators to see previous and subsequent frames while working on the current frame. Implement this feature to help users maintain consistency in their animations.

Playback and Preview

Include playback controls that allow users to preview their animations at different speeds and in a loop. A real-time preview of the animation as it progresses between keyframes can be highly beneficial.

Keyframe Management

Implement features for adding, removing, and duplicating keyframes. Users should be able to copy the properties of one keyframe to another for efficiency.

Undo and Redo

Include undo and redo functionality for keyframe actions. This ensures that users can experiment with their animations without fear of losing their work.

Storage and Export

Ensure that keyframes and their associated properties are stored efficiently to allow for saving and loading animations. Consider supporting common animation file formats for export.

Performance Considerations

Keyframe animation can be computationally intensive, especially with a large number of keyframes and complex interpolations. Optimize the rendering process to ensure smooth playback even for lengthy animations.

Incorporating keyframe animation into your 2D animation studio is a significant step toward making it a powerful tool for animators. In the next section, we will explore the management of animation timelines and sequences, which is essential for creating complex animations.

Section 18.3: Managing Animation Timelines and Sequences

Managing animation timelines and sequences is a critical aspect of building a 2D animation studio. In this section, we will explore how to create a user-friendly interface for handling timelines and sequences, allowing animators to organize and structure their animations effectively.

Understanding Timelines and Sequences

Before diving into implementation, let's clarify the concepts of timelines and sequences:

- **Timeline:** A timeline represents the entire duration of an animation project. It includes all the animation frames from the beginning to the end. Timelines provide a global view of the animation.

- **Sequence:** A sequence is a portion of the timeline that specifies which frames are used in a particular scene or shot. Sequences allow animators to work on different parts of the animation independently. For example, you might have one sequence for the introduction, another for a character's dialogue, and yet another for the closing credits.

To manage timelines and sequences effectively, your animation studio should include the following user interface components:

1. Timeline View

The timeline view is where users can see the entire project's timeline. It should display keyframes, markers, and sequences. Users should be able to zoom in and out to adjust the level of detail displayed.

2. Sequence Editor

The sequence editor allows animators to define sequences by specifying their start and end frames on the timeline. Sequences should be visually represented on the timeline view.

3. Sequence List

Provide a list or panel where users can see all the sequences in their project. They should be able to select a sequence to work on it or modify its properties.

4. Sequence Properties

Allow users to set properties for each sequence, such as its name, description, and any specific settings. For example, a sequence for a character's dialogue may have different settings than a sequence for a special effects scene.

Functionality

Here are some key functionalities to implement for managing timelines and sequences:

Creating Sequences

- Allow users to create new sequences and specify their start and end frames on the timeline.

Editing Sequences

- Enable users to modify the properties of existing sequences, such as changing their names or descriptions.

Organizing Sequences

- Implement features for rearranging sequences in the list or on the timeline, making it easy to adjust the order of scenes.

Navigating the Timeline

- Provide controls for quickly navigating through the timeline, such as playhead controls, frame jump buttons, and the ability to set markers.

Locking Sequences

- Allow users to lock sequences to prevent accidental changes while working on other parts of the animation.

Previewing Sequences

- Implement a preview feature that lets users preview individual sequences before rendering the entire project.

Exporting Sequences

- Enable users to export sequences as separate video files or image sequences for further editing or sharing.

Integration with Keyframe Animation

Integrate sequences with keyframe animation. When animators select a sequence, the timeline view should display only the frames within that sequence, making it easier to work on specific scenes.

Managing animation timelines and sequences effectively streamlines the animation creation process, especially for complex projects with multiple scenes. In the next section, we will explore advanced animation techniques to enhance the fluidity and realism of animations.

Section 18.4: Advanced Animation Techniques for Fluid Motion

In this section, we will delve into advanced animation techniques that will help achieve fluid and realistic motion in your 2D animations. Fluid motion is essential for creating lifelike and visually appealing animations, whether for games, films, or other multimedia applications.

1. Easing Functions**

Easing functions, also known as interpolation functions, control how an animation progresses between keyframes. Linear motion can appear robotic and unnatural. To achieve fluid motion, use various easing functions that simulate acceleration and deceleration. Common easing functions include ease-in, ease-out, ease-in-out, and custom bezier curves. You can apply these functions to position, rotation, scale, and other animation properties.

Here's an example of easing in CSS:

```css
/* Using ease-in-out easing function */
animation-timing-function: ease-in-out;
```

2. Motion Blur**

Motion blur is a visual effect that simulates the blurring of objects during fast motion. It adds realism and smoothness to animations. To implement motion blur, you'll need to render multiple frames with slight positional offsets between them and blend them together. The amount of blur depends on the speed and direction of the moving object.

Here's a simplified code snippet in Unity's ShaderLab to achieve motion blur:

```
// Vertex shader
v2f vert (appdata v)
{
    // Calculate new position with offset for motion blur
    float3 newPos = v.vertex.xyz + v.normal * _Speed * _Time;

    // Pass data to fragment shader
    v2f o;
    o.pos = UnityObjectToClipPos(newPos);
    return o;
}

// Fragment shader
half4 frag (v2f i) : SV_Target
{
    // Sample texture and apply motion blur
    half4 col = tex2D(_MainTex, i.uv);
    return col;
}
```

3. Secondary Motion**

Secondary motion refers to the additional movements that occur as a result of a primary motion. For example, when a character runs, their hair and clothing may sway. To achieve fluidity, simulate secondary motion by using physics simulations or procedural animations. This adds depth and realism to your animations.

4. Frame Blending**

Frame blending is a technique used in video editing and animation to smooth transitions between frames. It involves blending consecutive frames together to create intermediate frames. This technique can be useful for interpolating frames when working with lower frame rates or for adding a subtle smoothing effect.

In After Effects, for instance, you can enable frame blending for a layer to achieve this effect:

```
Layer > Frame Blending > Pixel Motion
```

5. Overlap and Follow-Through**

Overlap and follow-through are animation principles that contribute to fluid motion. Overlap occurs when different parts of an object move at slightly different times, creating a natural sense of weight and flexibility. Follow-through is the concept that after an object comes to a stop, certain parts of it (like hair or clothing) continue to move briefly.

Consider implementing these principles in your animations, especially for characters or objects with flexible components.

6. Realistic Physics**

If applicable to your animation, consider incorporating physics simulations. Tools like Unity's Physics2D engine or external physics libraries can help create lifelike movements for objects affected by gravity, collisions, and other forces.

Achieving fluid motion in 2D animations requires attention to detail and a combination of techniques. Experiment with easing functions, motion blur, secondary motion, frame blending, overlap and follow-through, and realistic physics to bring your animations to life. These techniques can be applied to character animations, object animations, and even special effects, enhancing the overall quality of your multimedia projects.

Section 18.5: Exporting Animations for Cross-Platform Playback

After you've created your 2D animations, it's essential to know how to export them effectively for cross-platform playback. Ensuring compatibility across various devices and software is crucial for reaching a broad audience and making the most of your multimedia projects. In this section, we'll explore the best practices for exporting animations in a cross-platform context.

1. File Formats**

Choosing the right file format is the first step in ensuring cross-platform compatibility. The two most common formats for 2D animations are GIF and APNG (Animated Portable Network Graphics). However, modern alternatives like WebP and MP4 are gaining popularity due to their better compression and support for higher-quality animations.

Here's how you might export an animation to WebP using FFmpeg:

```
ffmpeg -i input.gif -vf "scale=1280:-1" -c:v libwebp -lossless 1 output.webp
```

2. Resolution and Scaling**

Consider the target platforms and devices when determining the resolution of your animations. You may need to create multiple versions of your animation at different resolutions to accommodate various screen sizes and densities. Be mindful of aspect ratios and use vector-based graphics where possible to allow for scaling without loss of quality.

3. Frame Rate**

Maintaining a consistent frame rate is essential for smooth playback. The standard frame rate for animations is 24 or 30 frames per second (FPS). However, for web-based animations, 60 FPS might be preferable. Adjust the frame rate based on your target platform and intended visual style.

4. Compression**

Optimize your animation files by compressing them appropriately. Compression reduces file size without significantly compromising quality. Popular compression tools for animations include Gifsicle for GIFs, ImageMagick for various formats, and FFmpeg for video-based formats. Always test your compressed animations to ensure they maintain their visual integrity.

5. Metadata and Descriptions**

Include metadata and descriptions in your animation files. This information helps identify the content and provides context for users and developers. It's particularly important for accessibility and SEO (Search Engine Optimization). Metadata may include titles, descriptions, keywords, and copyright information.

6. Testing Across Platforms**

Before finalizing your animations, thoroughly test them on a variety of platforms and devices. Check for compatibility with different browsers, operating systems, and playback software. Ensure that the animations load correctly and play smoothly. Address any issues that arise during testing.

7. Cross-Platform Delivery**

Determine the best method for delivering your animations to your target audience. Depending on your project, this might involve embedding animations directly in web pages, packaging them with mobile apps, or distributing them through video-sharing platforms. Choose the delivery method that aligns with your project's goals and audience.

8. Accessibility Considerations**

Ensure that your animations are accessible to users with disabilities. Provide alternatives or descriptions for non-text content within animations, such as audio descriptions or subtitles. This ensures that everyone can enjoy your multimedia content.

9. Version Control and Backup**

Implement version control and backup strategies to protect your animation files. Use version control systems like Git to track changes and collaborate with team members. Regularly back up your animation files to prevent data loss.

10. Documentation**

Document the export process and file formats used for each animation. This documentation helps maintain consistency and assists other team members who may work on the project in the future. Include information about compression settings, frame rates, and any custom configurations.

In conclusion, exporting animations for cross-platform playback requires careful consideration of file formats, resolution, frame rate, compression, metadata, testing, delivery methods, accessibility, version control, and documentation. By following these best practices, you can ensure that your animations look and perform their best across a wide range of platforms and devices, maximizing their impact and reach.

Chapter 19: Advanced Artificial Intelligence in Games

Section 19.1: Developing Complex AI Behaviors

Artificial Intelligence (AI) plays a crucial role in modern video games, enhancing the player experience by creating intelligent and challenging opponents. Developing complex AI behaviors requires a deep understanding of AI techniques, algorithms, and game design principles. In this section, we'll explore the process of creating sophisticated AI behaviors that can make your games more engaging and immersive.

1. Understanding Game AI

Before diving into AI development, it's essential to understand the specific requirements and goals of your game. Consider the type of game you're creating, whether it's a strategy game, first-person shooter, or role-playing game, as this will influence the AI's behavior. Identify the challenges and interactions players will face, and design AI that complements these aspects.

2. Decision-Making Algorithms

One of the core components of game AI is decision-making. AI characters need to make decisions based on the game's context, their goals, and the player's actions. Various algorithms can be used for decision-making, including finite state machines (FSMs), behavior trees, and utility-based systems. Choose the one that best fits your game's requirements.

3. Pathfinding and Navigation

For AI characters to move intelligently within the game world, you'll need robust pathfinding and navigation systems. Techniques like A* and navigation meshes can help AI agents find the most efficient paths to their destinations while avoiding obstacles. Implementing dynamic pathfinding that adapts to changes in the environment is also essential for realistic AI behavior.

4. Sensing and Perception

AI characters should be aware of their surroundings and the player's actions. Implement sensory systems that allow AI to detect the player's presence, hear sounds, or see objects in their field of view. Combining different types of sensors, such as vision, hearing, and touch, can create more realistic and challenging AI opponents.

5. Learning and Adaptation

To make AI behaviors more dynamic, consider incorporating learning and adaptation mechanisms. Machine learning techniques, like neural networks or reinforcement learning, can allow AI to improve its performance over time. AI that adapts to the player's strategies or learns from its mistakes can create a more engaging gaming experience.

6. Balancing Difficulty

Balancing AI difficulty is a crucial aspect of game design. The AI should present an appropriate level of challenge, neither too easy nor too difficult. Implement difficulty levels or dynamic difficulty adjustment systems that adapt the AI's behavior based on the player's skill level and progression through the game.

7. Playtesting and Iteration

Developing complex AI behaviors is an iterative process. Constantly playtest your game to assess the AI's performance and fine-tune its behavior. Gather feedback from players and use it to make adjustments and improvements. Iteration is key to achieving the right balance and ensuring that the AI enhances the overall gaming experience.

8. Realistic Behaviors and Personality

Consider giving AI characters distinct personalities and behaviors that align with their in-game roles. Whether it's brave soldiers, cunning enemies, or timid NPCs, crafting realistic and believable behaviors can immerse players in the game world. Pay attention to details like animations, dialogue, and interactions.

9. Memory and Planning

For AI characters to make intelligent decisions, they should have a form of memory and planning. Implement systems that allow AI to remember past events, anticipate future actions, and strategize accordingly. Memory can be used for tracking the player's actions, storing preferences, and adapting strategies.

10. AI and Multiplayer Games

In multiplayer games, AI can serve various purposes, from providing solo challenges to acting as teammates or opponents. Consider how AI interacts with human players and design behaviors that enhance the multiplayer experience. Ensure that AI remains competitive and fair in multiplayer scenarios.

In conclusion, developing complex AI behaviors in games involves a combination of decision-making algorithms, pathfinding, sensing, learning, balancing, playtesting, personality, memory, and adaptation. By carefully crafting AI that suits your game's genre and objectives, you can create more engaging, challenging, and immersive gaming experiences that captivate players and keep them coming back for more.

Section 19.2: Integrating Machine Learning for AI Improvement

Integrating machine learning (ML) techniques into game development can significantly enhance AI behaviors by allowing AI characters to learn and adapt from their experiences. In this section, we'll explore how to integrate machine learning into game AI to create more intelligent and dynamic opponents.

1. Types of Machine Learning for Game AI

There are several types of machine learning that can be integrated into game AI:

- **Supervised Learning:** In supervised learning, AI agents learn from labeled data. For game AI, this could involve training AI to recognize specific player behaviors or patterns in the game environment.

- **Reinforcement Learning:** Reinforcement learning is particularly useful for game AI. AI agents learn by receiving rewards or punishments based on their actions. Over time, they discover optimal strategies through trial and error.

- **Unsupervised Learning:** Unsupervised learning can be applied to create AI behaviors that are less predictable. AI agents can learn to cluster and categorize game data without explicit labels.

2. Data Collection and Preprocessing

To train machine learning models for game AI, you'll need data. This data could include player actions, game states, and environmental information. Collecting and preprocessing this data is essential for training ML models effectively.

3. Building the ML Model

Select an appropriate machine learning framework or library for building your models. Popular choices include TensorFlow, PyTorch, and scikit-learn. Define the architecture of your model, which may involve neural networks, decision trees, or other ML algorithms, depending on the task.

4. Training the AI Agent

Training your AI agent involves exposing it to game scenarios and allowing it to learn. During training, the AI agent will receive data from the game and update its internal model based on the machine learning algorithm you've chosen. Training can take a significant amount of time and computational resources.

5. Reward Systems and Reinforcement Learning

In reinforcement learning, designing a proper reward system is crucial. Define rewards that encourage the AI agent to exhibit desired behaviors. For example, in a game, the AI might receive positive rewards for completing objectives or negative rewards for failing tasks.

6. Fine-Tuning and Evaluation

After training, it's essential to fine-tune your AI agent. Evaluate its performance in different game scenarios and adjust its behavior as needed. You may need to iterate on the training process several times to achieve the desired level of AI proficiency.

7. Real-Time Learning

In some cases, it's possible to implement real-time learning, where AI agents continue to learn and adapt during gameplay. This can lead to dynamic and evolving AI behaviors, making the game more engaging.

8. Balancing AI Learning

Balancing AI learning is critical to avoid situations where AI becomes too challenging or too predictable. Implement mechanisms to control the rate of learning or adapt the AI's behavior based on the player's skill level.

9. Data Privacy and Security

Consider data privacy and security when collecting and using player data for training AI. Ensure that you comply with relevant regulations and protect players' sensitive information.

10. Examples of ML-Enhanced Game AI

Machine learning-enhanced game AI can take various forms, such as NPCs that learn from player strategies, dynamic enemy behaviors that adapt to the player's style, or procedurally generated content that is tailored to the player's preferences.

By integrating machine learning into your game development process, you can create AI characters and opponents that continuously improve and provide players with engaging and challenging experiences. Keep in mind that implementing ML for game AI requires a deep understanding of both game design and machine learning principles, but the results can be highly rewarding in terms of player immersion and enjoyment.

Section 19.3: Adaptive AI Strategies and Player Behavior Analysis

In this section, we'll delve into the concept of adaptive AI strategies in game development and explore how analyzing player behavior can lead to more engaging and challenging gameplay experiences. Adaptive AI refers to AI systems that can adjust their behavior in response to how players interact with the game.

1. Understanding Adaptive AI

Adaptive AI is a technique that allows AI-controlled entities in a game to adapt to the player's actions, making the gameplay experience more dynamic and challenging. Instead of following predefined scripts, adaptive AI can make decisions on the fly based on the player's behavior.

2. Player Behavior Analysis

To implement adaptive AI, you first need to analyze player behavior. This involves gathering data on how players interact with your game. Some common metrics to consider include:

- **Player Movement:** Track how players move through the game world. Are they exploring every corner or rushing through?

- **Decision-Making:** Analyze the choices players make. Do they prefer stealthy approaches or direct combat?

- **Success and Failure Patterns:** Identify which sections of the game are causing players the most difficulty or where they excel.

- **Time Spent:** How long do players spend in different areas or on specific tasks?

- **Preferred Weapons or Abilities:** Determine which weapons or abilities players use most frequently.

3. Implementing Adaptive AI Strategies

Once you've gathered data on player behavior, you can use this information to inform your adaptive AI strategies. Here's how you can implement adaptive AI:

- **Behavior Trees:** Use behavior trees or similar systems to define AI behaviors. Based on player behavior data, you can adjust the probabilities of different branches in the tree, making certain behaviors more likely.

- **Dynamic Difficulty Adjustment (DDA):** Alter the game's difficulty in real-time based on player performance. If a player is struggling, you can reduce the number of enemies or provide hints. Conversely, if they're finding it too easy, you can increase challenges.

- **Player Modeling:** Create models of player behavior and adapt AI responses accordingly. For example, if a player is known to be aggressive, AI opponents can be more defensive when facing them.

- **Pattern Recognition:** Implement algorithms that recognize specific player behavior patterns. For instance, if a player consistently uses a particular strategy, the AI can devise counter-strategies.

4. Balancing and Fairness

It's crucial to strike a balance between challenging players and providing a fair and enjoyable experience. Overly aggressive adaptive AI can frustrate players, while overly passive AI can make the game too easy. Continuously playtest and fine-tune your adaptive AI to ensure it strikes the right balance.

5. Feedback and Communication

Consider providing players with feedback about the adaptive AI's behavior adjustments. This transparency can enhance the player experience. For example, you can display messages like "The AI has adapted to your aggressive playstyle" or "The AI is adjusting to your preference for stealth."

6. Player Choice and Agency

While adaptive AI can make games more engaging, it's essential to ensure that players still have agency and that their choices matter. Don't make AI adjustments feel like they're taking control away from the player. Instead, let players see the consequences of their actions.

7. Privacy and Ethics

Collecting player behavior data raises privacy and ethical considerations. Be transparent about data collection, anonymize data, and ensure compliance with relevant regulations, such as GDPR.

8. Examples of Adaptive AI in Games

Games like "Left 4 Dead" adjust the difficulty based on player performance, ensuring that challenges remain balanced. In "F.E.A.R.," enemy AI adapts to the player's tactics, making each encounter feel unique. "The Director" in "Left 4 Dead" is a prime example of dynamic difficulty adjustment, while "Alien: Isolation" showcases adaptive AI that learns the player's hiding spots.

Implementing adaptive AI requires a deep understanding of player psychology and behavior analysis. However, when executed well, it can greatly enhance the replayability and immersion of your games, providing players with more satisfying and personalized experiences.

Section 19.4: Advanced Pathfinding and Navigation Algorithms

In this section, we will explore advanced pathfinding and navigation algorithms used in game development. Efficient pathfinding is crucial for creating immersive and challenging game worlds where characters and entities can navigate intelligently.

1. Importance of Pathfinding

Pathfinding is the process of finding the most efficient route from one point to another while avoiding obstacles. In games, pathfinding is used by AI-controlled characters, enemies, and even non-playable characters (NPCs) to navigate game environments.

2. A* Algorithm

One of the most popular pathfinding algorithms in game development is the A*
(pronounced "A star") algorithm. A* is a heuristic search algorithm that efficiently finds the
shortest path from a starting point to a goal while considering the cost of movement.

```
# A* pseudocode
open_set = {start}
came_from = {}
g_score = {start: 0}
f_score = {start: g_score[start] + heuristic(start, goal)}

while open_set is not empty:
    current = node in open_set with the lowest f_score
    if current == goal:
        return reconstruct_path(came_from, current)
    open_set.remove(current)

    for neighbor in neighbors(current):
        tentative_g_score = g_score[current] + distance(current, neighbor)
        if tentative_g_score < g_score[neighbor]:
            came_from[neighbor] = current
            g_score[neighbor] = tentative_g_score
            f_score[neighbor] = g_score[neighbor] + heuristic(neighbor, goal)
            if neighbor not in open_set:
                open_set.add(neighbor)

return failure
```

3. Grid-Based Navigation

For grid-based game environments, A* works exceptionally well. Each cell in the grid
represents a navigable area, and obstacles are usually defined as impassable cells. A*
traverses the grid efficiently, making it ideal for tile-based games.

4. NavMesh Navigation

In more complex and irregular game environments, developers often use navigation
meshes (NavMeshes). A NavMesh is a simplified representation of the game world,
consisting of polygons where characters can move. Navigation algorithms like A* can be
applied to NavMeshes, allowing for realistic movement in intricate environments.

5. Dynamic Obstacle Avoidance

In dynamic game worlds, obstacles and entities can move. Pathfinding algorithms must
adapt to these changes in real-time. One way to handle dynamic obstacles is to use
techniques like the "Dynamic A*" algorithm, which updates paths when obstacles move.

6. Hierarchical Pathfinding

For large game worlds, hierarchical pathfinding can significantly reduce computation time. It involves breaking the world into smaller regions and generating paths between these regions. Then, A* is used to navigate within each region. This approach reduces the number of nodes A* needs to evaluate.

7. Behavior Tree Integration

In game AI, pathfinding is often integrated into behavior trees. Behavior trees determine what actions AI characters should take, including movement. When combined with pathfinding algorithms, behavior trees allow AI characters to make intelligent navigation decisions.

8. User-Friendly Tools

Game engines often provide user-friendly tools for defining navigation areas, obstacles, and AI behavior. These tools allow level designers and developers to create complex, dynamic, and believable game worlds without diving deeply into code.

9. Conclusion

Advanced pathfinding and navigation algorithms are vital for creating engaging and realistic game experiences. Game developers can choose from a variety of techniques, including the A* algorithm, grid-based navigation, NavMeshes, dynamic obstacle avoidance, hierarchical pathfinding, and behavior tree integration. The choice depends on the specific game requirements and the complexity of the game world. Mastery of these techniques is essential for game developers aiming to create immersive and challenging gameplay environments.

Section 19.5: Creating AI-Driven Storytelling in Games

In this section, we will delve into the fascinating realm of AI-driven storytelling in games. Advanced artificial intelligence (AI) techniques are employed to create dynamic, player-responsive narratives that enhance immersion and replayability.

1. The Role of AI-Driven Storytelling

AI-driven storytelling aims to break away from linear narratives and offer players a more interactive and personalized experience. Instead of following a predetermined script, players' choices and actions shape the unfolding story. This approach provides players with a sense of agency and investment in the game world.

2. Branching Narrative Systems

One common technique for AI-driven storytelling is the use of branching narrative systems. In this approach, the game's narrative is represented as a tree-like structure, with each node representing a story event or decision point. Player choices dictate which path the narrative takes, leading to different outcomes.

```
// Example of a branching narrative structure
{
  "start": {
    "text": "You find yourself in a dark forest. Do you go left or right?",
    "options": [
      {
        "text": "Go left",
        "leads_to": "left_path"
      },
      {
        "text": "Go right",
        "leads_to": "right_path"
      }
    ]
  },
  "left_path": {
    "text": "You discover a hidden treasure chest.",
    "options": []
  },
  "right_path": {
    "text": "You encounter a ferocious dragon!",
    "options": []
  }
}
```

3. Dynamic Character Interactions

AI-driven storytelling also involves dynamic character interactions. Non-playable characters (NPCs) in the game world have their own goals, motivations, and personalities. AI algorithms govern how these characters react to the player's actions and decisions, allowing for complex and realistic interactions.

```
# Pseudocode for NPC behavior
if player_talks_to_npc:
    if player_has_item("quest_item"):
        npc_says("Thank you for finding my lost item!")
        npc_gives_reward()
    else:
        npc_says("I have a task for you. Can you find my lost item?")
        npc_assigns_quest("find_lost_item")
```

4. Procedural Content Generation

To keep the narrative fresh and engaging across multiple playthroughs, AI-driven storytelling often incorporates procedural content generation. This technique creates new story elements, characters, and quests procedurally, ensuring that no two playthroughs are exactly the same.

5. Learning and Adaptation

Advanced AI-driven storytelling systems can learn from player behavior and adapt the narrative accordingly. Machine learning algorithms can analyze player choices and preferences, allowing the game to tailor the story to individual players.

6. Player-Character Alignment

Another intriguing aspect of AI-driven storytelling is player-character alignment. The game AI can assess the player's decisions and adjust the player character's personality, moral compass, or alignment to align more closely with the player's choices.

7. Challenges in AI-Driven Storytelling

While AI-driven storytelling offers immense potential, it comes with challenges. Designing coherent narratives with meaningful choices, managing branching complexity, and ensuring player agency without compromising narrative quality are among the key challenges faced by game developers.

8. Conclusion

AI-driven storytelling represents a significant advancement in game design, enabling dynamic and player-responsive narratives. Branching narrative systems, dynamic character interactions, procedural content generation, learning and adaptation, and player-character alignment are all integral to creating compelling AI-driven narratives. Game developers looking to engage players with immersive and personalized storytelling experiences should explore these techniques and adapt them to their games' unique requirements. AI-driven storytelling holds the promise of revolutionizing the way players experience and interact with game narratives, offering infinite storytelling possibilities.

Chapter 20: Cross-Platform AR and VR Experiences

Section 20.1: Introduction to Augmented Reality (AR) and Virtual Reality (VR)

In this final chapter, we explore the exciting world of augmented reality (AR) and virtual reality (VR) experiences, focusing on their cross-platform development with SFML. AR and VR are immersive technologies that have the potential to transform the way we interact with digital content and the physical world. By understanding the fundamentals of AR and VR development and how to make them cross-platform using SFML, developers can create captivating and innovative applications that span multiple devices and platforms.

1. Understanding Augmented Reality (AR)

Augmented reality (AR) overlays digital content onto the real world, enhancing our perception and interaction with our surroundings. AR applications often use devices like smartphones, tablets, or AR glasses to blend computer-generated elements with the user's view of the physical world. Examples of AR applications include interactive museum exhibits, navigation apps with AR directions, and games like Pokémon GO.

2. Exploring Virtual Reality (VR)

Virtual reality (VR) immerses users in a completely digital environment, shutting out the physical world to create a simulated reality. VR experiences are typically delivered through headsets that provide a 360-degree view of a virtual world. VR applications range from immersive gaming and simulations to virtual tours and training scenarios.

3. Cross-Platform Development with SFML

SFML's cross-platform capabilities make it a valuable tool for AR and VR development. Whether you're targeting smartphones, tablets, desktops, or even VR headsets, SFML provides a consistent framework for graphics, input, and audio, simplifying the development process. Additionally, SFML's extensibility allows developers to integrate AR and VR hardware and libraries effectively.

4. Building AR Applications with SFML

To develop AR applications with SFML, developers can leverage camera input and sensor data from AR-capable devices. SFML's graphics and rendering capabilities can be used to overlay digital content onto the camera feed, creating immersive AR experiences. Additionally, SFML's support for touch and gesture input is beneficial for building interactive AR applications.

```cpp
// Example code for overlaying digital content in AR
void renderARScene(sf::RenderWindow& window, sf::Texture& cameraFeed, sf::Sprite& digitalContent) {
    // Capture camera feed
    sf::Texture cameraTexture;
```

```
    cameraTexture.loadFromImage(getCameraImage()); // Function to obtain came
ra image
    sf::Sprite cameraSprite(cameraTexture);

    // Overlay digital content
    window.draw(cameraSprite);
    window.draw(digitalContent);

    // Display the composite image
    window.display();
}
```

5. VR Development and Interaction with SFML

When developing VR applications with SFML, the focus shifts to creating fully immersive experiences. SFML can be used to render stereoscopic 3D scenes and handle VR headset input for head tracking and user interaction. Integrating SFML with VR SDKs like SteamVR or Oculus SDK allows for seamless cross-platform VR development.

```
// Example code for VR headset integration
void handleVRInput(sf::RenderWindow& window) {
    // Get VR headset input
    sf::Event event;
    while (window.pollEvent(event)) {
        if (event.type == sf::Event::Closed) {
            window.close();
        }
        // Handle VR input events
    }
}
```

6. Cross-Platform AR/VR Deployment and Compatibility

Deploying AR and VR applications across different platforms can be challenging due to hardware variations and software dependencies. Developers must consider compatibility with various AR glasses, VR headsets, and operating systems. SFML's cross-platform nature eases the deployment process, but thorough testing and adaptation may still be required.

7. Exploring Future Trends in AR and VR Multimedia

The field of AR and VR is continuously evolving, with new hardware, software, and use cases emerging regularly. Developers should stay updated with the latest trends and innovations, such as augmented reality contact lenses, mixed reality experiences, and advanced haptic feedback systems, to create cutting-edge AR and VR applications.

8. Conclusion

As we conclude this book, we've journeyed through the advanced techniques and applications of the Simple and Fast Multimedia Library (SFML). From advanced graphics rendering and game development to cross-platform coding and AI-driven storytelling, you've gained a comprehensive understanding of how SFML can empower your multimedia projects.

In this final chapter, we explored the immersive worlds of augmented reality (AR) and virtual reality (VR) and how SFML can be used to create cross-platform AR and VR experiences. With the knowledge gained from this book, you are well-equipped to embark on your own multimedia development adventures, pushing the boundaries of what's possible in the world of interactive and immersive content. The future of multimedia programming is bright, and SFML is your gateway to it.

Section 20.2: Building AR Applications with SFML

Augmented Reality (AR) is a technology that overlays digital content onto the real world, providing interactive and enhanced experiences. Building AR applications with SFML is an exciting venture, as it allows developers to harness the library's powerful graphics and input capabilities for creating immersive AR experiences. In this section, we will delve into the process of building AR applications using SFML.

Understanding AR Development with SFML

To create AR applications with SFML, it's crucial to grasp the fundamental concepts and workflow:

1. **Camera Feed Integration:** AR applications typically require access to the device's camera feed. SFML provides support for capturing camera input, making it possible to overlay digital content onto the live camera view.

2. **Graphics Rendering:** SFML's robust graphics rendering capabilities enable developers to seamlessly blend digital elements with the camera feed. You can use SFML's `sf::Sprite` and `sf::Texture` to display and manipulate AR content.

3. **User Interaction:** Interactivity is a key aspect of AR applications. SFML allows you to handle touch input, gestures, and user interactions effectively, enhancing the user's experience.

Basic AR Application Workflow

Let's outline the basic workflow for creating a simple AR application with SFML:

1. **Initialize SFML:** Start by initializing SFML components, including the window, camera access, and any necessary resources such as textures and models.

2. **Capture Camera Feed:** Use SFML to access the device's camera and continuously capture frames from it. You can achieve this by creating a camera feed texture and updating it with each frame.

```
// Example code for capturing camera feed
sf::Texture cameraFeed;
```

```cpp
sf::Sprite cameraSprite;

while (window.isOpen()) {
    // Capture camera frame
    sf::Image cameraFrame = captureCameraFrame(); // Implement this function
    cameraFeed.loadFromImage(cameraFrame);

    // Update camera sprite
    cameraSprite.setTexture(cameraFeed);

    // Render camera feed and AR content
    window.clear();
    window.draw(cameraSprite);
    renderARContent(window); // Function to render AR elements
    window.display();
}
```

3. **Render AR Content:** Overlay digital content, such as 3D models or 2D images, onto the camera feed using SFML's rendering capabilities. Ensure that the AR content aligns correctly with the real-world scene.

```cpp
// Example code for rendering AR content
void renderARContent(sf::RenderWindow& window) {
    // Load AR content (e.g., 3D model)
    sf::Texture arTexture;
    arTexture.loadFromFile("ar_model.png");

    sf::Sprite arSprite(arTexture);

    // Position and scale the AR content based on real-world tracking
    arSprite.setPosition(100, 100); // Adjust position as needed
    arSprite.setScale(0.5f, 0.5f); // Adjust scale as needed

    // Draw AR content onto the window
    window.draw(arSprite);
}
```

4. **User Interaction:** Implement user interaction features, such as tapping on AR objects or recognizing gestures. SFML's input handling capabilities can be used to detect and respond to user actions.

5. **Cross-Platform Considerations:** While SFML simplifies cross-platform development, ensure that your AR application is compatible with various devices and operating systems. Test on different platforms and devices to address any compatibility issues.

6. **Performance Optimization:** Optimizing the performance of AR applications is crucial, especially when rendering complex 3D models. Utilize SFML's rendering optimizations and consider implementing techniques like occlusion culling to improve performance.

Conclusion

Building AR applications with SFML opens up a world of possibilities for creating interactive and immersive experiences that blend the digital and physical realms. By understanding the core concepts of AR development and leveraging SFML's capabilities, developers can embark on exciting projects that push the boundaries of augmented reality. Whether it's for gaming, education, or practical applications, SFML provides a versatile platform for AR development across different devices and platforms.

Section 20.3: VR Development and Interaction with SFML

Virtual Reality (VR) is a technology that immerses users in a completely digital environment, offering a sense of presence and interactivity. Developing VR applications with SFML is an exciting prospect as it allows developers to harness the library's capabilities to create immersive VR experiences. In this section, we will explore the process of VR development and interaction using SFML.

Understanding VR Development with SFML

Before diving into VR development with SFML, it's essential to comprehend the fundamental concepts and workflow involved:

1. **Head-Tracking:** VR relies heavily on head-tracking to provide a realistic sense of presence. Devices like VR headsets track the user's head movements, and SFML can be used to capture and interpret this data.

2. **Stereo Rendering:** VR applications typically require rendering two distinct views— one for each eye. SFML's graphics capabilities are well-suited for creating stereo-rendered scenes that align with the user's perspective.

3. **User Interaction:** Interaction in VR is often achieved through motion controllers or hand tracking. SFML can facilitate the integration of such input devices for interactive VR experiences.

Basic VR Application Workflow

Let's outline the basic workflow for creating a simple VR application with SFML:

1. **Initialize SFML:** Start by initializing SFML components, including the VR headset, rendering context, and any necessary resources such as textures and models.

2. **Head-Tracking Integration:** Capture head-tracking data from the VR headset to determine the user's viewpoint. SFML can be used to update the camera or render view based on the user's head movements.

```
// Example code for head-tracking integration
sf::RenderWindow window(sf::VideoMode(1920, 1080), "VR Application", sf::Styl
e::Fullscreen);
```

```cpp
while (window.isOpen()) {
    // Capture head-tracking data from VR headset
    sf::Vector3f headPosition = getHeadPosition(); // Implement this function
    sf::Vector3f headRotation = getHeadRotation(); // Implement this function

    // Update camera or render view based on head position and rotation
    updateVRView(headPosition, headRotation); // Implement this function

    // Render the VR scene
    renderVRScene(window); // Implement this function
}
```

3. **Stereo Rendering:** Configure SFML to render the scene from two perspectives—one for each eye of the user. This creates the stereoscopic effect necessary for a convincing VR experience.

```cpp
// Example code for stereo rendering
void renderVRScene(sf::RenderWindow& window) {
    // Set up left-eye view
    sf::View leftEyeView = window.getDefaultView();
    leftEyeView.setViewport(sf::FloatRect(0, 0, 0.5f, 1.0f)); // Left half of
the window
    window.setView(leftEyeView);

    // Render left-eye view here

    // Set up right-eye view
    sf::View rightEyeView = window.getDefaultView();
    rightEyeView.setViewport(sf::FloatRect(0.5f, 0, 0.5f, 1.0f)); // Right ha
lf of the window
    window.setView(rightEyeView);

    // Render right-eye view here

    window.display();
}
```

4. **User Interaction:** Integrate motion controllers or hand tracking devices for user interaction. SFML's input handling capabilities can be employed to detect and respond to user actions within the VR environment.

5. **Cross-Platform Considerations:** Ensure compatibility with various VR headsets and platforms. SFML simplifies cross-platform development, but thorough testing is crucial to address compatibility issues.

6. **Performance Optimization:** VR applications demand high performance to maintain a smooth and immersive experience. Employ SFML's rendering optimizations and consider techniques like level of detail (LOD) for complex scenes.

Conclusion

Developing VR applications with SFML opens up exciting possibilities for creating immersive and interactive digital environments. By understanding the core concepts of VR development and leveraging SFML's capabilities, developers can embark on projects that transport users to virtual worlds. Whether for gaming, education, or simulation, SFML provides a versatile platform for VR development across different VR headsets and platforms, enabling the creation of captivating and engaging VR experiences.

Section 20.4: Cross-Platform AR/VR Deployment and Compatibility

Cross-platform deployment is a critical aspect of ensuring that your Augmented Reality (AR) and Virtual Reality (VR) experiences reach a wide audience. In this section, we'll explore the strategies and considerations for deploying AR and VR applications built with SFML on various platforms.

AR Deployment Considerations

Augmented Reality applications blend digital content with the real world, typically through mobile devices such as smartphones and tablets. Here are some considerations for deploying AR applications cross-platform:

1. **Platform Compatibility:** ARCore (for Android) and ARKit (for iOS) are two popular AR development platforms. When developing with SFML, you'll need to ensure that your application can seamlessly switch between these platforms, leveraging their respective AR capabilities.

2. **Device Support:** Not all mobile devices are AR-capable. It's essential to provide clear information to users about which devices and operating system versions are compatible with your AR app. You can also implement checks within your app to notify users if their device lacks AR support.

3. **Cross-Platform Libraries:** Utilize cross-platform libraries and frameworks that abstract the underlying AR platform differences. Such libraries can simplify AR app development and deployment.

4. **User Experience:** Design your AR app's user interface and interactions to be intuitive and user-friendly across different devices and screen sizes. Consider the varying capabilities of device cameras and sensors.

VR Deployment Considerations

Virtual Reality applications provide immersive experiences that often involve headsets and motion controllers. Deploying VR apps across platforms involves specific considerations:

1. **Headset Compatibility:** VR headsets vary significantly in terms of hardware and tracking technology. Ensure that your VR application supports a range of headsets, including popular ones like Oculus Rift, HTC Vive, and Windows Mixed Reality.

2. **Input Devices:** VR experiences heavily rely on motion controllers or hand tracking. Implement input handling in a way that accommodates different controller types and interaction methods.

3. **Performance Optimization:** VR applications demand high performance to maintain frame rates and reduce motion sickness. Optimize your app's rendering and interactions to achieve smooth experiences on various VR-ready PCs.

4. **Distribution Platforms:** Decide on the distribution platform for your VR app. Popular choices include SteamVR, Oculus Store, and Windows Store. Each platform may have specific requirements and guidelines for submission.

5. **Cross-Platform Development:** Leverage SFML's cross-platform capabilities to simplify VR app development. Test your app thoroughly on different VR platforms to ensure compatibility and performance.

6. **User Comfort:** Consider the comfort of VR users. Provide options for adjusting graphics settings, controlling motion sensitivity, and setting play area boundaries to enhance user comfort and safety.

Testing and Quality Assurance

Thorough testing is crucial for cross-platform AR and VR deployment. Test your application on a variety of devices, operating systems, and headsets to identify compatibility issues and ensure a consistent user experience. Address any platform-specific bugs or performance bottlenecks before releasing your app to a broader audience.

Conclusion

Deploying AR and VR applications built with SFML on multiple platforms requires careful planning and consideration of platform-specific requirements and user experiences. By addressing compatibility, performance, and user comfort, you can offer engaging AR and VR experiences to a wide range of users, whether they're using smartphones for AR or high-end PCs for VR. Additionally, leveraging cross-platform development tools and libraries can streamline the deployment process and help you reach a broader audience with your immersive applications.

Section 20.5: Exploring Future Trends in AR and VR Multimedia

Augmented Reality (AR) and Virtual Reality (VR) are dynamic fields that continually evolve with technological advancements and changing user expectations. In this section, we'll explore some of the future trends and innovations expected in AR and VR multimedia.

1. Enhanced Interactivity

Future AR and VR experiences will focus on enhancing interactivity. This includes more advanced hand tracking, gesture recognition, and natural language processing to create immersive and intuitive user interfaces. Users can expect to interact with digital objects and environments more naturally, making the experiences feel even more lifelike.

2. Improved Graphics and Realism

Advancements in hardware, such as more powerful GPUs and higher-resolution displays, will lead to significantly improved graphics and realism in AR and VR. This will result in more detailed and convincing virtual environments, making users feel like they are truly part of the experience.

3. Integration with AI and Machine Learning

AI and machine learning technologies will play a more prominent role in AR and VR applications. AI-driven content generation, adaptive storytelling, and personalized experiences are areas where these technologies will shine. AI will also assist in real-time object recognition and tracking, enhancing the interaction between the digital and physical worlds.

4. Spatial Audio and 3D Soundscapes

Audio is a critical component of immersive experiences. Future AR and VR systems will focus on spatial audio, creating 3D soundscapes that match the visual environments. This will not only improve realism but also enhance user engagement and help with spatial awareness.

5. Cross-Platform Integration

As AR and VR become more mainstream, there will be a greater emphasis on cross-platform integration. Users will expect seamless transitions between AR and VR experiences on different devices, from smartphones and tablets to VR headsets and AR glasses. Developing for multiple platforms will become even more critical.

6. Health and Safety Innovations

User comfort and safety will continue to be a priority. Future AR and VR systems will feature advanced technologies to reduce motion sickness, such as improved motion tracking and reduced latency. Additionally, health monitoring features may be integrated into AR glasses and VR headsets to ensure users' well-being during extended usage.

7. Educational and Training Applications

AR and VR have immense potential in education and training. In the future, we can expect to see more educational content and immersive training simulations. These technologies will enable hands-on learning experiences in fields like medicine, engineering, and more.

8. Social and Collaborative AR/VR

Collaborative AR and VR experiences will become more common, allowing users to interact with others in shared virtual spaces. Social platforms and virtual meeting spaces will see significant growth, transforming how people connect and collaborate over long distances.

9. Sustainable and Eco-Friendly Solutions

Environmental considerations will also play a role in the future of AR and VR. Innovations in sustainable hardware design and energy-efficient algorithms will help reduce the carbon footprint of AR and VR technologies, making them more eco-friendly.

10. Privacy and Ethical Concerns

As AR and VR collect more data about users and their environments, privacy and ethical concerns will become more prominent. Future developments will need to address these issues, including data security, user consent, and responsible data usage.

In conclusion, the future of AR and VR multimedia is bright and full of exciting possibilities. With advancements in hardware, AI, and user experience design, these technologies will continue to push boundaries, offering users increasingly immersive and interactive experiences. As developers and creators, staying informed about these trends and innovations will be essential for crafting compelling AR and VR content in the years to come.